100

THINGS TO DO IN

TEXAS

BEFORE YOU

DIE

100

THINGS TO DO IN
TEXAS
BEFORE YOU
DIE

E. R. BILLS

REEDY PRESS

Library of Congress Control Number: 2018945695

ISBN: 9781681061832

Design by Jill Halpin

Printed in the United States of America
18 19 20 21 22   5 4 3 2 1

Please note that websites, phone numbers, addresses, and company names are subject to change or cancellation. We did our best to relay the most accurate information available, but due to circumstances beyond our control, please do not hold us liable for misinformation. When exploring new destinations, please do your homework before you go.

DEDICATION

This book is dedicated to my parents,
E. R. Bills Sr. and Rebecca Sue Bills.
They gave me a big head start.

CONTENTS

• •

Parks and Recreation

• •

• •

Food and Drink

Road Trips

• •

Photo Ops

● ●

ACKNOWLEDGMENTS

Special thanks to the family, friends, and fellow Texans who inspired or informed my travels or helped me put this volume together, including my wife, Stacie, my children, Alta and Johnnie Kettler, Ron Howell, Billy Huckaby, Kathy Hudson, Michael H. Price, Scot Courtney, Scott Conner, Dale Stockstill, Jonna and Durren Anderson, Sarah Cortez, and too many others to name.

PREFACE

When you get right down to it, there's no way of avoiding criticism for limiting a premortem bucket list of "things to do in Texas before you die" to a measly one hundred. John Steinbeck was correct when he asserted that "Texas is the obsession, the proper study, and the passionate possession of all Texans," and anyone who's lived here ten years can easily rattle off a hundred things they'd like to do before they finish their lunch break.

The challenge, then, is looking over the entire state and narrowing down which settings and activities are the most germane in terms of Texas culture or a true Texas experience. This does not mean ranking activities around the state with an eye on their popularity or how easy they are to reach. A hard look is required, and even then it's tough to narrow down what's intrinsically Lone Star.

I am a native Texan and have resided in Texas all my life. I began traveling the state early. When I was twelve, my father took my younger brother and me on an eight-day canoe trek down the Lower Canyons of the Rio Grande, and the experience has never left me. For the last twenty years or so, I've explored almost every corner of the state myself, at times solo, with my wife, with my wife and kids, and sometimes just with the kids. We've gotten muddy on wild cave tours, ventured down the entire length of the sixty-mile Padre Island National Seashore, shared a beach with a nesting Kemp's ridley sea turtle, witnessed the

Perseid meteor shower while standing in the South Llano River, attended the Ghost Walk in Jefferson, snuck down the Ghost Road of Saratoga, had the Devil's River all to ourselves, seen black bears in the Big Bend, stumbled across secret weapons at the Devil's Sinkhole, kept time with Cassiopeia at the McDonald Observatory, examined the Buried City in the Panhandle, leaped off limestone cliffs at Inks Lake, navigated Caddo Lake, drove the free golf carts around Fort Griffin, braved the City Tube Chute in New Braunfels (without a tube), petted stingrays at the Texas State Aquarium, and been emphatically warned by the heart-stopping hiss of a mama alligator at Sea Rim. We've defeated electronica for significant spells, confounded GPS, gone days without a cell phone signal, and wandered into places where it seemed there wasn't another human being for a hundred miles. We've explored our home state with vim and vigor and had countless epiphanies, revelations, and breathtaking moments of sheer, unbridled joy at the breadth, depth, and diversity of this place, which is why I feel comfortable attempting this list.

—E. R. Bills

• •

AMUSEMENTS AND ENTERTAINMENT

EXPLORE
THE SAN ANTONIO RIVERWALK

Now comprising fifteen miles of pedestrian paths that hug the San Antonio River's edge, the Riverwalk stretches from the community's art center to its fabulous Spanish missions, which are a must-see in their own right. Shaded by the surrounding buildings, the river winds through the busy downtown commerce area, plied by colorful cruise barges and tour-guide gondoliers. The spectacle gives San Antonio one of the best downtowns in America and easily the best in Texas. There's nothing else quite like it.

Spend a day or an evening or two or three of each. Take in the sights and sounds and people. You'll understand why everyone is smiling.

www.thesanantonioriverwalk.com

GO TO LUCKENBACH ...

There's no greater testament to the power of a country song than the tiny Hill Country community of Luckenbach. Founded in the mid-nineteenth century and virtually a ghost town by the early 1970s, Luckenbach was a place folks saw no reason to stop in for decades. But then Waylon Jennings (who'd never been to Luckenbach) and Willie Nelson recorded and released "Luckenbach, Texas (Back to the Basics of Love)," and bingo! A speck on the map with only three permanent residents was transformed into one of the epicenters of the country music universe.

And so it remains today.

If you call yourself a Texan, it's hard to argue against a pilgrimage to Luckenbach at your earliest convenience. The town's two remaining businesses are the general store (which moonlights as a saloon and a post office) and the dance hall. The general store is a good place to grab a beer and pick out a souvenir—it sells Luckenbach bumper stickers, ball caps, bandanas, patio bricks, coffee mugs, and coozies. The store website features a busy events calendar all year round and has a link to the monthly *Luckenbach Moon* newsletter, where you can survey a month-to-month schedule of upcoming musical acts and general goings-on.

412 Luckenbach Town Loop
Fredericksburg, TX 78624
(830) 997-3224
www.luckenbachtexas.com

MILL AROUND
IN MARFA

Ever wonder what a meeting between hipster bohemians and West Texas might look like? Marfa provides the answer.

The eighty-eight-year-old Hotel Paisano is now a ritzy rendezvous point for starched-jean ranch hands and globetrotting South Americans, Asians, Germans . . . all in search of a latte on the frontier. Throw in a thrift store (the only one for a hundred miles in any direction), several Manhattan-priced art galleries, a woke food truck, and El Cosmico—a hostel-like spread of community accommodations that offers space in trailers, teepees, safari tents, yurts, and a 3,800-square-foot apartment on the second floor of the Brite Building downtown (for large group rental)—and this little town delivers an inimitable atmosphere of quirkiness that serves as an entertaining break from conventional West Texas fare. Sometimes you get the feeling the place is full of folks who wanted to visit West Texas but not really *be* in West Texas, but that's all right.

Yes, there's a coffee shop (Frama), a bookstore (Marfa Book Company), a hip rustic bar, and random beer gardens. Oh, and those world-famously fickle Marfa Lights.

www.visitmarfa.com

GET WET
AT THE TEXAS STATE AQUARIUM

The largest aquarium in Texas and one of the largest in the United States, the Texas State Aquarium may be the best attraction to visit on the entire Gulf Coast. A self-supporting, nonprofit institution dedicated to promoting environmental conservation and the rehabilitation of wildlife in the Gulf of Mexico, the facility is located at the southernmost tip of the bayside Corpus Christi Beach.

Ever petted a shark before?

What about a starfish or a stingray?

Visitors can get up close and personal with all sorts of sea life here, including sea otters, sea turtles, groupers, tuna, and invertebrate Medusozoa—jellyfish. The big fish tank is stunning, and the vertical tank jellyfish exhibits are practically otherworldly. A small water park is also out front for young folks.

2710 N. Shoreline Blvd.
Corpus Christi, TX 78402
(800) 477-4853
www.texasstateaquarium.org

INTREPID TEXAN
The *Mirador de la Flor*, a monument to slain Tejano music superstar Selena Quintanilla Perez, sits just a few minutes away at 600 N. Shoreline Blvd.

TAKE IN A RODEO

When Greenville native Audie Murphy—the most decorated American soldier of World War II—was asked about the true meaning of America, he gave a short list of things that he thought summed us up. The list ended with the sound of children laughing, a newspaper, a political rally, and a policeman's badge. The list started with a Texas rodeo.

A Texas rodeo may or may not encapsulate the true meaning of America, but it definitely captures some of the authentic essence of the Lone Star State. Texas wasn't an easy place to live in the old days, and it wasn't for the faint of heart. The early residents and settlers—white, brown, black, and red—were hardscrabble, tough customers. They had to be. The desolate frontier was an unpredictable, unforgiving place, and the modern rodeo still celebrates the pioneer side of our forebears' hardships.

West of the Pecos Rodeo (last weekend in June)
The real deal and attracts professional rodeo
cowboys from all over the country

Pecos, TX
www.pecosrodeo.com

Texas Cowboy Reunion (usually late June or early July)
Known as the "World's Largest Amateur Rodeo"

U.S.-277, Stamford, TX 79553
www.texascowboyreunion.com

Stockyards Championship Rodeo (weekly)
Held every Friday and Saturday night, the world's
first indoor rodeo and only year-round rodeo

Cowtown Coliseum
121 E. Exchange Ave.
Fort Worth, TX 76164
www.stockyardsrodeo.com

San Antonio Stock Show & Rodeo (in February)
One of the largest rodeos in the world

723 AT&T Center Pkwy.
San Antonio, TX 78219
www.sarodeo.com

**Houston Livestock Show & Rodeo
(late February through mid-March)**
Another one of the largest rodeos in the world

Houston, TX
www.rodeohouston.com

EAT OR COMPETE
AT THE TERLINGUA CHILI COOKOFF

Tex-Mex and BBQ may be the heavy hitters in terms of the Lone Star palate—but don't say that in front of chili folks. Chili is a formidable Texas dish in its own right and makes a good case for a Lone Star culinary trifecta, especially since, to date at least, our big chili cookoff earns much more acclaim and renown than our BBQ contests. In fact, the Terlingua Chili Cookoff is actually two chili cookoffs held in the same town at the same time. The Original Terlingua International Championship Chili Cookoff and the Chili Appreciation Society International's Texas International Chili Championship commence simultaneously in late October and end in early November. Both events offer chili options galore and bring in musical acts for entertainment.

www.abowlofred.com
www.casichili.net/terlingua-273604.html

INTREPID TEXAN
The Terlingua Trading Company is an excellent resource for Big Bend souvenirs and general Texana, and it sits right next to the Starlight Café.

TWO-STEP
AT THE BROKEN SPOKE

Long before Austin was weird or anyone was even trying to keep it weird, the Broken Spoke was just country. Now that Austin is clearly becoming more corporate than weird, the Spoke, unaffected by the hipster chic springing up around it, is weirdly even more country.

A roadhouse dance hall that's probably one of the few places left in Austin where you can still really find Texas, the Spoke has hosted most of the country greats over the years, including Bob Wills and the Texas Playboys, Tex Ritter, Ernest Tubb, Roy Acuff, Kitty Wells, Willie Nelson, Asleep at the Wheel, and George Strait, who appeared there once a month from 1975 to 1982. The 661-person capacity venue still showcases old-time country music, serves good food and cold beer, and may be the best place in the state to two-step.

3201 S. Lamar Blvd.
Austin, Texas 78704
(512) 442-6189
www.brokenspokeaustintx.net

INTREPID TEXAN
In the event that you might enjoy a break from old-time country music or two-stepping, there's always Sixth Street, which lends credibility to the claim that Austin is the Live Music Capital of the World, and it's lined with the largest number of prospective pubs and bars to crawl of any community in the land.

OTHER LIVE MUSIC VENUES

Gruene Hall
Texas's oldest dance hall

1281 Gruene Rd., New Braunfels, TX 78130
(830) 606-1281
www.gruenehall.com

John T. Floore's Country Store
Storied honky-tonk venue with BBQ and an outdoor stage

14492 Old Bandera Rd., Helotes, TX 78023
(210) 695-8827
www.liveatfloores.com

Cheatham Street Warehouse
Laidback heavyweight that has hosted Willie Nelson,
Jerry Jeff Walker, Townes Van Zandt, Marcia Ball, and
many more; also gave George Strait and the Ace in the
Hole Band their first gig, booked Stevie Ray Vaughan
for a long-running weekly appearance, and developed
legendary alt-country folk artist Todd Snider

119 Cheatham St., San Marcos, TX 78666
(512) 353-3777
www.cheathamstreet.com

McGonigel's Mucky Duck
Modern pub and music venue featuring
the "Livest Music in Texas"

2425 Norfolk St., Houston, TX 77098
(713) 528-5999
www.mcgonigels.com

Austin City Limits Live at the Moody Theater
A recorded PBS event; the longest-running
music program in television history

310 West Willie Nelson Blvd., Austin, TX, 78701
(512) 225-7999
www.3tenaustin.com

VISIT A GHOST TOWN

There's no getting around the growing urbanization of the Lone Star State, and this trend has been unmistakably detrimental to small towns, the more traditional underpinnings of Texas culture. Love it or hate it, Texans have become citified, and the skeletal remains created by this perhaps inevitable phenomenon—ghost towns—will probably continue to increase in number. They dot the state in every direction, and they're important to look upon as Texans reconcile with who they were and what they're becoming. Some communities died overnight, and others took years to kill. Many were the result of unsustainable industrial development, and others suffered catastrophes. Some simply perished at the whim of a railroad route preference or highway planning. Regardless of the details, they are poignant reminders of things past and eloquent harbingers of things to come.

SOME GHOST TOWNS TO VISIT

Thurber

Located in Palo Pinto County, just north of the intersection of State Hwy. 108 and Interstate 20. The nearby W. K. Gordon Center for Industrial History of Texas lies in the area and offers a case study of Thurber's rise and decline.

Kent

Located in Culberson County at the intersection of CR 2424 and Interstate 10, Kent is still on maps, but only an abandoned convenience store, a few empty houses, and the rock walls of a large, gutted public school remain.

Independence

The wealthiest community in the state in 1845, Independence was the original site of Baylor University and Sam Houston's home when he served as a U.S. senator. When town leaders refused to grant a right-of-way to the Santa Fe Railroad, it took its tracks elsewhere, and Independence began a slow decline. A few buildings and markers and four columns from the original Baylor University edifice still remain.

Tascosa

Located in Oldham County just north of the intersection of U.S. Hwy. 385 and Ranch to Market Rd. 1061, Tascosa (or Old Tascosa) sprang up in the 1880s as a good stop on the way to Dodge City, Kansas. It briefly served as the capital of ten Texas Panhandle counties and became a regional merchandising center for ranches within a hundred-mile radius. The only two structures left are the remains of a crumbling rock schoolhouse (erected in 1889) and the old courthouse (now the Julian Bivins Museum), both of which are part of Cal Farley's Boys Ranch.

FILL YOUR STEIN
AT WURSTFEST

Wurstfest in New Braunfels is one of the grandest celebrations of German culture in the United States, bringing together all kinds of Texans with several generations of their German neighbors. For ten consecutive days, folks from all over pour into the Comal County community's Landa Park to fill their beer steins to the brim with German beer and consume copious amounts of German sausage. There's wurst stew, wurst on a roll or stick, sauerkraut, deep-fried sauerkraut balls, strudels, *kartoffelpuffer* (potato pancakes), and polka music.

Founded in 1961, the first Wurstfest attracted two thousand people. Today, the event attracts more than one hundred thousand participants. Bring a hardy appetite, reduced culinary inhibitions, and your favorite pair of lederhosen. *Prost!*

STARGAZE
AT THE MCDONALD OBSERVATORY

Commencing at an open-air amphitheater about a half hour after sunset in the Davis Mountains, the Evening Star Parties at the McDonald Observatory (held Tuesdays, Fridays, and Saturdays, with additional nights added during peak season) are one of the coolest things to do in Texas. Resident astronomers use laser pointers to identify prominent stars, planets, and constellations in the night sky and then treat attendees to incredible views of galaxies, supernovas, and other celestial bodies in some of the observatory's high-powered telescopes. The observatory also offers daytime solar viewings and guided tours of the facility, and the visitors center includes exhibits, a theater, and a gift shop.

3640 Dark Sky Dr.
Fort Davis, TX 79734
(432) 426-3640
www.mcdonaldobservatory.org

INTREPID TEXAN
The Chihuahuan Desert Nature Center is just twenty miles away on State Hwy. 118. It's an excellent resource for examining regional flora.

www.cdri.org

WATCH
YOUR FAVORITE SPORTS TEAM PLAY

Like everywhere else in America, sports are a big deal in Texas, and most folks feel pretty strongly about their favorite teams at the professional and college levels. Even when wildly disparate Texans cannot, will not, and never agree on a single political or philosophical question, they become tight-knit, "take-a-bullet-for-you" brothers (or sisters) at the tailgate party on game day.

The Dallas Cowboys are still America's team. Houston is finally getting over the loss of the Oilers and embracing the Texans. The Houston Astros are coming off a World Series championship. The San Antonio Spurs have won five NBA championships and currently hold the highest all-time NBA regular season win-loss record percentage. Then, of course, there's the Dallas Mavericks, the Houston Rockets, the WNBA's Dallas Wings, the Dallas Stars, F.C. Dallas, and the Houston Dynamo.

At the college level, fans are no less tribal, but most Texans bleed Aggie maroon or Longhorn burnt orange.

INTREPID TEXAN
More than four thousand roller derby clubs can be found across America, and Austin has its own four-team league known as the Texas Rollergirls.

www.texasrollergirls.org/teams-staff

Dallas Cowboys
AT&T "Jerryworld" Stadium
1 AT&T Way
Arlington, TX 76011
www.attstadium.com

Houston Texans
NRG Stadium
1 NRG Pkwy.
Houston, TX 77054

San Antonio Spurs
AT&T Center
1 AT&T Center Pkwy.
San Antonio, TX 78219
www.attcenter.com

Houston Rockets
Toyota Center
1510 Polk St.
Houston, TX 77002
www.houstontoyotacenter.com

Dallas Mavericks/ Dallas Stars
American Airlines Center
2500 Victory Ave.
Dallas, TX 75219
www.americanairlinescenter.com

Houston Astros
Minute Maid Park
501 Crawford St.
Houston, TX 77002
www.houston.astros.mlb.com/
hou/ballpark/index.jsp

Texas Rangers
Globe Life Park in Arlington
1000 Ballpark Way
Arlington, TX 76011
www.mlb.com/rangers

Texas A&M University
Kyle Field
756 Houston St.
College Station, TX 77843
www.12thman.com/
facilities/?id=1

University of Texas
Darrell K. Royal–Texas
Memorial Stadium
405 E. Twenty-Third St.
Austin, TX 78712
www.texassports.com/
sports/2013/7/24/facilities_
0724133148.aspx?id=205

ATTEND THE STATE FAIR
OF TEXAS

Staged at historic Fair Park on the outskirts of Dallas, the State Fair of Texas is an exciting sensory overload. The smell of fresh, deep-fried corny dogs (where they were actually invented); the culinary array of other deep-fried whatsits you're tempted to try after the corny dog; the clatter, laughter, and buzz of people playing games at the Texas-sized midway; the amusements and rides, including a roller-coaster and the twenty-story, thirty-five-gondola Ferris wheel (the tallest in the state); a stock show and strange animal races; the cookoffs, the live music and the wine garden; and Big Tex welcoming all, even after the Texas-OU game. *Win or lose.*

The twenty-four-day event was first held in 1886 and usually begins every year on the last Friday in September.

3921 Martin Luther King Jr. Blvd.
Dallas, TX 75210
(214) 565-9931
www.bigtex.com

INTREPID TEXAN
If you have any energy left after the fair, an interesting evening can be had in Deep Ellum, Dallas's eclectic downtown entertainment district.

FLOAT A RIVER

It's hard to get more Texan than floating a river. Most of the state is hot most of the year, and at one time or another most Texans have tried to find ways to cool off. Utilizing an old inflated truck or tractor tire inner tube was a stroke of genius back in the early days, and now you can find inflatable vinyl tubes for purchase or rent at most river float destinations. Heck, today you can even put your hands on deluxe, two-passenger inflatable tubes (in any color), a tow-along tube for your ice cooler, and electric tube inflators. But it's still about the water, the sun, and a gaggle of like-minded river rats (and triple-digit SPF sunscreen before or half-inch-thick slathers of after-sun lotion after—if you forget).

Guadalupe River
It is practically a Texas pilgrimage.

Guadalupe River State Park
3350 Park Rd. 31
Spring Branch, TX 78070
www.tpwd.texas.gov/state-parks/guadalupe-river

San Marcos River
Put in at Sewell Park, it runs through the
Texas State University campus.

Sewell Park
601 University Dr.
San Marcos, TX 78666
www.campusrecreation.txstate.edu/outdoor/sewell-park.html

South Llano River
A great three-quarter-mile stretch lies in the South Llano
River State Park, but you can put in at one or two bridges
farther down U.S. Hwy. 377 and make a day of it.

South Llano River State Park
1927 Park Rd. 73
Junction, TX 76849
www.tpwd.texas.gov/state-parks/south-llano-river

City Tube Chute
Big fun with the tube or without, but
without is not for the faint of heart.

100 Liebscher Drive
New Braunfels, TX 78130
(830) 608-2165
www.nbtexas.org/1438/City-Tube-Chute

Frio River
Almost three prime miles of the Frio
meander through Garner State Park.

234 RR 1050
Concan, TX 78838
www.tpwd.texas.gov/state-parks/garner

TAKE A STROLL
ON THE GALVESTON SEAWALL

Morning, noon, or night, the seawall in Galveston is a Lone Star marvel. Almost seventeen feet tall and sixteen feet thick (at the base), this protective barrier runs for more than ten miles—the mainland side lined with restaurants, hotels, bars, and souvenir shops, and the beach side occasionally intersected by a jetty or fishing pier. Intermittent stairs allow access to the beach and Gulf of Mexico, but the sidewalk path on the wall gives you a view of it all—wall, beach, water, and so much more. It's a beautiful pedestrian byway that's sure to inspire some good memories.

At the intersection of Twenty-Fifth St. and Seawall Blvd., visitors find the Galveston Historic Pleasure Pier (which extends out over the ocean), a perfect platform for carnival games, several rides, a small roller-coaster, and a large Ferris wheel.

INTREPID TEXAN
The Galveston downtown area has some real spunk. Check out the Strand District, Bishop's Palace, the Nautical Antiques and Tropical Decor shop, and the Galveston Bookshop.

CREATE GRAFFITI
AT THE CADILLAC RANCH

Amarillo's Cadillac Ranch, a row of ten used Cadillacs buried nose-first in the ground at an angle that corresponds to the Great Pyramid at Giza (Egypt), was created by the Ant Farm, an avante-garde architecture collective. Founded in San Francisco in the late 1960s, the Ant Farm got busy in the early 1970s, creating inexpensive, portable, vinyl shelters known as inflatables for progressive forums and communal "happenings." Their world-famous Cadillac Ranch was completed with the assistance of Amarillo eccentric Stanley Marsh 3 in 1974 and probably says something subversive about the iconic Cadillac and American pop culture, but most folks just spray paint on a Caddy or two (there's a Home Depot right down the road) and take pictures.

Which is your cue, graffiti or no.

13651 I-40 Frontage Rd.
Amarillo, TX 79124

INTREPID TEXAN

On I-27 heading south out of Amarillo, two gigantic legs jut vertically from a concrete base. They are known as "Ozymandias on the Plains" and are also a Stanley Marsh 3–backed art installation.

STEP ABOARD
THE TEXAS STATE RAILROAD

Writer G. K. Chesterton once remarked that "the only way of catching a train I have ever discovered is to miss the train before." In the infancy of the new millennium, most Texans have missed the era of railroad travel by a few generations and will probably never be able to fully appreciate it for what it was, but we can still catch a glimpse of it in the Piney Woods of East Texas.

The Texas State Railroad still operates four steam engines over one hundred years old and makes runs from Rusk to Palestine on a regular basis, with several passenger options. For $85, you can travel Presidential Class and enjoy appetizers and complimentary champagne. First Class runs $65, and Open-Air Coach (featuring vintage wooden seats) runs $45. For $300 you can join the engineer up front for a ride-along.

535 Park Rd. 76
Rusk, TX 75785
(855) 632-7729
www.texasstaterailroad.school

FEEL THE NEED
FOR SPEED

Though Texas is known for many things, speed is rarely high on the list. This may be a grievous oversight.

The first "fastest man alive" was Gainesville native Charles Paddock. He captured a silver medal in the 200 meters and gold in the 100 meters and 4×100-meter relay at the 1920 Olympics and inspired future Olympian Jesse Owens, who won four gold medals at the 1936 Olympics. In the 1956 Olympics, San Benito native Bobby Morrow duplicated his hero Jesse Owens's medal counts in the sprint events. More recently, Texas has produced Michael Johnson, Carlette Guidry, Jeremy Wariner, and Courtney Okolo and developed transplants such as Carl Lewis and Sanya Richards-Ross.

The annual Clyde Littlefield Texas Relays (held at the University of Texas in Austin) is the second-largest track meet in America. It begins during the first or second week in April and features high school, college, and professional athletes from around the world. If you're looking for speed, the Texas Relays is where it's at.

Mike A. Myers Stadium
707 Clyde Littlefield Dr.
Austin, TX 78705
www.relays.texassports.com

SEE JEFFERSON

This Marion County treasure near the eastern edge of Texas is tough to beat for a weekend getaway. The weekly Ghost Walk, mostly conducted in the well-preserved downtown, is wildly entertaining (even for skeptics). You can test your mettle by staying in a haunted hotel (Excelsior House) or visit the Grove, which is hands-down (or flailing at your side as you flee) the most haunted place in Texas.

The charming town is also home to the nostalgic Jefferson General Store, the fascinating Jefferson Historic Museum, the historic House of the Seasons, a *Gone with the Wind* museum, and one of the last remaining Carnegie libraries (that's still in operation) in Texas.

Jefferson also offers access to swamp tours, bayou tours, and great fishing at Caddo Lake or Lake O' Pines. Is your overnight bag ready yet?

INTREPID TEXAN

Wiley College, home of the "Great Debaters," is only seventeen miles south on U.S. Hwy. 59 in the city of Marshall.

GET MODERN
IN FORT WORTH

The fifteenth-largest city in the United States, Fort Worth (a.k.a. Cowtown), is the cowboy-est of all major American cities, but the big ranchers who drove the growth of the community aspired to a degree of sophistication as well. In the short term, these aspirations manifested themselves in parlor room pianos and a market for piano vendors. In the long term, they fostered a piano virtuoso named Lee Van Cliburn, which led to Fort Worth becoming host of one of the most prestigious classical music events in the world, the quadrennial Van Cliburn International Piano Competition.

Early businesspeople followed the ranchers' lead, and today Fort Worth is home to three museums that make it an international art mecca of the first order. The Kimbell Art Museum sits in what is considered one of the state's foremost works of modern architecture and makes the itinerary for any serious art buff. The permanent collection features works by Rembrandt, Monet, and Picasso. The Amon Carter Museum of American Art houses one of the world's best collections of American art, including works by Winslow Homer, Edward Hopper, and Frederic Remington. The Modern Art Museum holds one of the most important collections of modern and contemporary art in the United States, displaying works by Picasso, Warhol, Jackson Pollock, and Francis Bacon.

www.kimbellart.org
www.cartermuseum.org
www.themodern.org

CELEBRATE
CINCO DE MAYO

Often mistaken for Mexico's Independence Day, Cinco de Mayo actually celebrates the Mexican army's unlikely defeat of the sneaky French at the Battle of Puebla on May 5, 1862.

While Texans and Americans were embroiled in the Civil War, Napoleon III decided to establish a French empire in Mexico. A large French force landed at Veracruz and vanquished it relatively easily. Then they began marching inland toward Mexico City, and an unofficial, quasi-Texan intervened. The vastly outnumbered Mexican forces were led by Ignacio Zaragoza, a general and politician who was born in 1829 in a Mexican community that later became known as Goliad (in the Republic and state of Texas). As soil hardly knows the difference, Zaragoza is a Tex-Mex hero at the very least, and we should laud his historic victory. Without it we might be addicted to Franco-Tex instead of Tex-Mex.

So drink some Dos Equis (or Negra Modelo, Tecate, Pacifico, or Corona), grab some tacos, attend one of the parades, and celebrate one of *our* heroes.

MOSEY UP TO THE BAR
IN A TEXAS SALOON

A Texan may not have invented beer drinking or bars, but Texans have perfected the former and ardently support the latter. Texas is, after all, home to Shiner Bock, Pearl Beer, Rahr & Sons, and too many new craft beers to name. The state even has a beer named after it: Lone Star.

Texans have also been known to imbibe lugubrious amounts of tequila, which you'd think we invented (especially considering the massive quantities of it consumed herein), and margaritas, which some cocktail historians maintain was invented here in 1948 at the Balinese Room in Galveston.

A good way to tell when a Texan has drunk too much?

When he or she is drinking out of his or her own boot.

Menger Hotel Bar
One of the top ten most historic bars in the United States

204 Alamo Plaza
San Antonio, TX 78205
(210) 223-4361

White Elephant Saloon
The site of high-stakes poker games and several gunfights
in the early days and still a Cowtown favorite

106 E. Exchange Ave.
Fort Worth, TX 76102
(817) 624-8273

Devil's Backbone Tavern
Immortalized by alt-folk singer-songwriter Todd Snider in
"The Story of the Ballad of the Devil's Backbone Tavern"

4041 Farm to Market 32
Fischer, TX 78623
(830) 964-2544

Lone Star Saloon
Opened in 1955 and located in the heart of downtown Houston

1900 Travis St.
Houston, TX 77002
(713) 757-1616

11th Street Cowboy Bar
The biggest little bar in Texas and bras hang from the ceiling

307 Eleventh St.
Bandera, TX 78003
(830) 796-4849
www.11thstreetcowboybar.com

ATTEND A TEXAS FESTIVAL

This is a tough one because they come in all shapes, sizes, venues, and themes and, in a place as big as Texas, you have hundreds to choose from. From SXSW, Bat Fest, and Eeyore's Birthday Party honoring Winnie the Pooh's friend—all in Austin—to a celebration of salt in Grand Saline, a Stone Age Fair in Perryton, and a watermelon thump in Luling, the Lone Star State has something to satiate any festival fetish.

SOME TEXAS FESTIVALS

Kerrville Folk Festival (Kerrville)
Since 1972, folk music for eighteen days and nights

www.kerrvillefolkfestival.org

Nacogdoches Film Festival (Nacogdoches)
Since 2011, a great, local, intimate event where you
can rub elbows with some established film sorts

www.nacogdochesfilmfestival.com

Great Texas Mosquito Festival (Clute)
Since 1981, its mascot a twenty-five-foot inflatable
mosquito dubbed Willie Man-Chew; enough said

www.mosquitofestival.com

Luling Watermelon Thump (Luling)
Since 1953, includes watermelon thumping, watermelon
seed spitting, a Thump Queen, and a thumping parade

www.newsite.watermelonthump.com

Parker County Peach Festival (Weatherford)
Since 1984, a nostalgic, peachy procession that includes a
bike ride, live music, more than two hundred arts, crafts,
food, and activity booths, and a "42" domino tourney

www.parkercountypeachfestival.org

Texas Rose Festival (Tyler)
Since 1933, a celebration of the rose industry
in Tyler, featuring a rose parade, coronation,
talent show, and arts and crafts fair

www.texasrosefestival.com

Charro Days (Brownsville)
Since 1937, the biggest celebration in the Rio
Grande Valley; includes great food, big sombreros,
street dancing, a carnival, and a costume ball

www.charrodaysfiesta.com

TAKE A FRIEND
TO TRY THE 72-OUNCE BIG TEXAN
CHALLENGE

Aspiring gorgers have one hour to consume this massive Big Texan Steak Ranch & Brewery beef bomb and all the fixins, which include a shrimp cocktail, a baked potato, a salad, and a roll. The $72 cost of the meal must be paid up-front, and that amount is refunded if the challenge is completed. Don't expect a reenactment of the boiled egg scene from *Cool Hand Luke* because all takers have to cut the steak themselves and feed themselves. Once an attempt has started, ambitious eaters can't get up or leave the table. If a participant can consume the entire meal in sixty minutes or less, they emerge victorious and are immortalized forever in the coveted Big Texan 72oz Hall of Fame.

7701 Interstate 40 Access Rd.
Amarillo, TX 79118
(806) 372-6000
www.bigtexan.com

INTREPID TEXAN
Don't make the mistake of thinking size matters in this contest. The current record is held by a 125-pound female competitive gorger who actually finished two Big Texan challenges in the allotted one-hour time frame.

BUY THE PERFECT TEXAS SOUVENIR

It's true that you can buy a one-inch salt crystal at the Salt Palace in Grand Saline or a piece of the meteorite that formed the crater at the Odessa Meteor Crater and Museum, but those are awfully specific and not generally recognized in regard to Texas. Then there's the Alamo snow globe, which obviously says Texas—but was clearly devised by folks who never lived here.

What says "Hello . . . I've been to Texas"?

In terms of jewelry, a Concho pearl (typically pink or purple), native to the Concho River near San Angelo. If a fashion statement is the aim, get handmade boots or a ten-gallon hat. To elicit a *What the heck?* response—bring home a Día de los Muertos skull. And if you just want to say in a friendly way, "I'm cooler than you," pick up a six-pack of Shiner Bock.

EXPERIENCE
A BIG BEND STATE OF MIND

More than any other park, site, place, or activity, the Big Bend echoes a popular Texas mantra: It's a state of mind. The roads widen, and the days stretch out. Time expands, and it's impossible to get anywhere fast. Big Bend National Park is as big as the entire state of Rhode Island and a three- or four-day visit hardly scratches the surface.

Protecting more than 1,000 species of flora, at least 450 species of birds, 56 species of reptiles, and 75 species of mammals, this 801,163-acre spread is a national park system rock star. Mountains, desert, forest, river, hot springs, dinosaur bones, fossilized sea creatures, volcanic dykes, black bears, mountain lions, hiking, biking, canoeing, kayaking, camping on high ground, camping on low ground—you really can't get your head around it until you've been there, and once you've been there you can't stop going back.

The thirteen-mile South Rim Trail is one of the best hikes in the world, but the tough Emory Peak Trail, the picturesque Lost Mine Trail, the Boquillas Canyon Trail (down to the Rio), the dramatic Santa Elena Trail, the stark Ernst Tinaja hike, and even the kooky Grapevine Hills jaunt are all sublime. The easy Hot Springs hike near Rio Grande Village is always in order after one of the longer treks (remember to bring a towel).

The drives are equally impressive, and you can also book overnight canoe or kayak excursions through Santa Elena Canyon. The park-maintained campsites in the Chisos Basin and the primitive campsites scattered throughout the terrain can be reserved, and if you plan far enough ahead you can get good air-conditioned accommodations at the Chisos Mountain Lodge.

Don't put this off. The Big Bend is big and intimidating, but around these parts, it's a peerless landscape for the adventurous.

www.nps.gov/bibe
www.nps.gov/bibe/planyourvisit/campground_reservations.htm
www.chisosmountainslodge.com

INTREPID TEXAN

The Tuff Canyon Trail just before the Castolon Visitor Center on the way to Santa Elena Canyon is a nice little hike and worth a stop.

HIKE
THE GUADALUPE MOUNTAINS NATIONAL PARK

Few views are as majestic as the Guadalupe Mountains approached on a clear day from the west or staring out and around once atop the 8,751-foot Guadalupe Peak. From the west, you encounter the Guadalupe Mountains as a sky island towering above a flat, white sand salt basin. From the peak itself, you see hundreds of miles of the Chihuahuan Desert in every direction. If the strenuous 8.4-mile round-trip hike to the peak doesn't fit into your plans, a quick half-mile jaunt into the western Salt Basin is fun, or you can visit the Pine Springs Visitor Center for information on other excursions, including the excellent (moderate) 6.8-mile round-trip McKittrick Springs Trail and the picturesque Devil's Hall.

The Guadalupe Mountains were sacred to the Apache, and some reportedly snuck back and remained after their official confinement to reservations. Rumors persist that their campsites and teepees were stumbled upon by visitors well into the early twentieth century.

You can find some excellent picnic spots on the way up to the visitors center, some good developed campsites once there, and, of course, primitive camping on the interior.

Pine Springs Visitor Center
400 Pine Canyon Dr.
Salt Flat, TX 79847
(512) 398-2712
www.nps.gov/gumo/planyourvisit/pine-springs-visitor-center.htm

GET LOST
ON CADDO LAKE

Just kidding. Because people do it every weekend.

Too many Texans (and Americans) view lakes simply as bodies of water created for perfecting their water sports acumen (including but not limited to waterskiing, wakeboarding, and jet skiing), and Caddo Lake is anathema to said mind-set. The snaking, meandering 26,000-acre Caddo Lake is like a primordial soup, in places densely forested, but everywhere teeming with life and thick with mystery. Legendary Eagles recording artist Don Henley was born in East Texas and has a property on Caddo. He says, "If there's any evidence of divinity on this Earth at all, it certainly exists here."

A significant number of ambitious landlubbers venture out onto the lake in canoes and kayaks during the daytime but find themselves lost as nightfall arrives. They wind up stuck there overnight, feasted on by mosquitoes and terrorized by howls of Bigfoot or whatever other creatures that prowl the Caddo after hours. If you're paddling out very far, play it safe and hire a guide.

www.captronswamptours.com

INTREPID TEXAN
Caddo Lake State Park offers good fishing opportunities and excellent camping and cabin accommodations.

www.tpwd.texas.gov/state-parks/caddo-lake

BEACHCOMB
PADRE ISLAND NATIONAL SEASHORE

The longest undeveloped stretch of public beach in the continental United States (sixty miles) and part of the longest undeveloped barrier island in the world, the 130,434-acre Padre Island National Seashore is a national treasure. Though plenty of beach lovers are always there, they congregate at the 5-mile and 10-mile marker points, camping, picnicking, sunbathing, swimming, body surfing, and shell hunting. The crowd gets scarce out past the 15- and 20-mile markers, and by the 25-mile marker you can have a wide swathe of beach to yourself. A four-wheel drive vehicle is recommended out past the 5-mile marker, and you'll have to bring along any food, drink, or camping gear you require. The weekly fee for this primitive stretch of paradise is $20. If your old VW van will still start, a yearlong stay runs $1,040!

Starting around the 15-mile marker, critically endangered Kemp's ridley sea turtles come up the beach and nest. A local, all-volunteer turtle patrol keeps a watchful eye and later makes sure the hatchlings make it out to sea.

Malaquite Visitor Center
20420 Park Road 22
Corpus Christi, TX 78418

INTREPID TEXAN

If you venture out just past the 50-mile marker at low tide, you can still spot the bulkhead of the SS *Nicaragua* about a hundred feet out. The 190-foot steamer ran ashore in 1912, and locals visited the wreck in their Model Ts for years afterward.

VISIT PALO DURO CANYON

Anyone who has spent much time around Texans knows they usually don't cotton to playing second, much less third, fiddle, but Mexico's Copper Canyon is the deepest and widest canyon in North America, and the Grand Canyon is the deepest and largest in the United States. Our Palo Duro Canyon is third to the former and second to the latter but no less spectacular. Approximately 120 miles long and several miles wide in places, Palo Duro has depths of up to 1,200 feet. In the Palo Duro Canyon State Park, the highlights include thirty miles of hiking trails, the popular Lighthouse Peak rock formation, and striated canyon walls highlighted with bright reds, yellows, and oranges. Artist Georgia O'Keeffe lived in the area in the early twentieth century and made use of Palo Duro as a subject, describing it as "a burning, seething cauldron, filled with dramatic light and color."

Palo Duro Canyon State Park
11450 State Hwy. Park Rd. 5
Canyon, TX 79015
(806) 488-2227
www.tpwd.texas.gov/state-parks/palo-duro-canyon

INTREPID TEXAN

The Texas Parks and Wildlife Department rents three Civilian Conservation Corps–built cabins on the Palo Duro Canyon rim, and they cannot be recommended highly enough in terms of location and views.

www.tpwd.texas.gov/state-parks/
palo-duro-canyon/fees-facilities/cabins

DIVE INTO
A TEXAS SWIMMING HOLE

Texas was recently called the swimming hole capital of the United States, and everyone around the country was surprised except those who live here.

In a place that stays as hot as Texas, every swimming hole offers an indispensable oasis where folks who are tough enough to stand the heat here can let their hair down and rejuvenate. In extreme cases, these reprieves are granted in the form of water troughs or stock tanks, but the best options are rivers, lakes, and spring-fed pools. Most of the top spots are in Central Texas, but you can also find a few refreshing standouts in East and West Texas.

The rest is simple. Jump in, cool off, and repeat as necessary.

SOME SWIMMING HOLES

Jacob's Well Natural Area
This is a beautiful little spot near Wimberley.

1699 Mt. Sharp Rd., Wimberley, TX 78676
(512) 214-4593
www.co.hays.tx.us/jwna.aspx

Hamilton Pool Preserve
Incredible natural grotto pool; call ahead for reservations.

24300 Hamilton Pool Rd., Dripping Springs, TX 78620
(512) 264-2740
www.parks.traviscountytx.gov/find-a-park/hamilton-pool

Devil's Waterhole, Inks Lake State Park
This refreshing pool is between pink granite
cliffs, perfect for swimming and cliff diving.

3630 Park Rd. 4 W, Burnet, TX 78611
(512) 793-2223
www.tpwd.texas.gov/state-parks/inks-lake

Tyler Lake, Tyler State Park
The diving raft is a great place for escaping
the heat in the Piney Woods.

789 Park Rd. 16, Tyler, TX 75706
(903) 597-5338
www.tpwd.texas.gov/state-parks/tyler

San Solomon Springs
Recently closed indefinitely due to earthquake damage related
to regional fracking; hopefully, it will be back up soon.

Balmorhea State Park
9207 TX-17
Toyahvale, TX 79786
(432) 375-2370
www.tpwd.texas.gov/state-parks/balmorhea

CLIMB ENCHANTED ROCK

A Lone Star version of Australia's Ayers Rock, the Hill Country's Enchanted Rock has enchanted locals and visitors for twelve thousand years. In the daytime, the pink granite batholith, which sits in the 1,643-acre Enchanted Rock State Natural Area, rises from the surrounding landscape somewhat unobtrusively, a subtle vertical anomaly; but at night it's known to groan and crackle as it cools down, converting humbugs and naysayers with equal aplomb.

A good short jaunt for regular hikers and a great slow slog for less seasoned outdoors partakers, the Summit Trail ascends forty stories in a little over a half mile, and when you arrive up high, you're treated to a terrific view and some perfect backdrop boulders. After you catch your breath, check out the Enchanted Rock Cave and Lunch Rock.

16710 Ranch Rd. 965
Fredericksburg, TX 78624
(830) 685-3636
www.tpwd.texas.gov/state-parks/enchanted-rock

INTREPID TEXAN
The informative National Museum of the Pacific War is only eighteen miles south on Ranch Road 965 in Fredericksburg, the hometown of Chester W. Nimitz, commander in chief of the U.S. Pacific Fleet in World War II.

CATCH A DUNE
AT THE MONAHANS SANDHILLS

Ever surf a sand dune? You can at the Monahans Sandhills State Park.

Located halfway between Odessa and Pecos, this 3,800-acre gem is home to thousands of dunes, some over seventy feet in height. The park headquarters rents sand-surfing disks and offers interpretive exhibits. The park itself has several picnic spots and more than two dozen campsites featuring the standard amenities.

The Monahans Sandhills are a great stop on any long trek across West Texas, but make sure you bring flip-flops and sunscreen.

2500 E. Interstate 20, Exit 86
Monahans, TX 79756
(432) 943-2092
www.tpwd.texas.gov/state-parks/monahans-sandhills

EXPLORE A TEXAS CAVERN

Texas caverns are an underutilized resource in terms of recreation and once-in-a-lifetime experiences. You can, of course, take the basic tours and spend an hour following a guide on a lighted, leisurely pathway ticking off the prescribed sights. There's nothing wrong with it, especially if you're too young, too old, or limited by health conditions; but if you aren't too young, too old, or physically limited, you should tackle some of the Wild or Adventure cave tours. Squeeze through narrow passages, cross low-ceiling stretches of limestone on your hands and knees, get a little scraped up and muddy—but don't hit, bump, or dislodge your head lamp. It gets awfully dark down there.

Longhorn Cavern State Park

Right down the road from Inks Lake State Park; the
two make a great summer day combination.

6211 Park Road 4 S
Burnet, TX 78611
(512) 715-9000
www.visitlonghorncavern.com

Caverns of Sonora

Check out the helictites and repel down a cavern chamber wall.

1711 Pvt Rd. 4468
Sonora, TX 76950
(325) 387-3105
www.cavernsofsonora.com

Kickapoo Cavern State Park

Primitive tours are available every Saturday,
but reservations are required.

20939 Ranch to Market Road 674
Brackettville, TX 78832
(830) 563-2342
www.tpwd.texas.gov/state-parks/kickapoo-cavern

Inner Space Cavern

Accidentally discovered by the Texas Highway
Department in 1963 during the construction of Interstate
35, this is one of the best preserved caves in Texas.

4200 N. Interstate 35 Frontage Rd.
Georgetown, TX 78626
(512) 931-2283
www.innerspacecavern.com

Natural Bridge Caverns

One of the largest cave complexes in the state;
the Watchtower and the Castle of White Giants steal the show.

26495 Natural Bridge Caverns Rd.
San Antonio, TX 78266
(210) 651-6101
www.naturalbridgecaverns.com

DISAPPEAR
IN THE DEVILS RIVER STATE NATURAL AREA

Forty-five miles from Del Rio and eighty miles from anywhere else, the most devilish aspect of the Devils River these days is getting to it. Once you spot the sign on the west side of U.S. Hwy. 277, you take a twenty-five-mile gravel road to the state natural area office, sign in, park a few miles farther down, and then hike a shadeless .93 miles to the river. At the end of the hike, you'll be tempted to jump in the river at the base of the last hill, but take a hard right instead and go another quarter mile or so. There the water winds along the limestone banks in Caribbean hues.

Most Texans never visit the Devils River State Natural Area, and that's a shame—but perhaps better for the hardy spirits who do. They have a spring-fed oasis to themselves, and less traffic means a better chance for the threatened species that live in the Devils River watershed to survive and thrive.

21715 Dolan Creek Rd.
Del Rio, TX 78840
(830) 395-2133
www.tpwd.texas.gov/state-parks/devils-river

DISCOVER
THE DEVIL'S SINKHOLE

Another neglected natural wonder in southwest Texas is the Devil's Sinkhole. When you first observe this sudden fifty-foot-wide, four-hundred-foot-deep opening in the Edwards Plateau, you think deer, stray horses, cattle, or other critters would have accidentally plunged to their deaths while in full flight when they encountered it, but the only victims seem to be rattlesnakes, which the fall doesn't always kill. Scientists have never discovered a large mammal bone in the sinkhole, but that may be because of the permanent residents. The sinkhole is home to several million Mexican free-tailed bats that emerge at sunset. The best time to see the bat show is from April through October.

The Devil's Sinkhole State Natural Area is a long way from the usual tourist attractions, but it's well worth a detour.

Devil's Sinkhole Society
101 N. Sweeten St.
Rocksprings, TX 78880
(830) 683-2287
www.tpwd.texas.gov/state-parks/devils-sinkhole

INTREPID TEXAN
The Devil's Sinkhole was cordoned off and protected by marines in the early 1940s because the bats there were utilized for a secret weapon that vied with the Manhattan Project to end World War II. Ask your sinkhole guide about Project X-Ray.

GREET AUTUMN
AT DAINGERFIELD STATE PARK

Texans have a special affinity for autumn. The cool late September breezes mean the furnace-like heat of summer has been turned off (or at least down), and the leaves will soon begin to take on bright colors. Daingerfield State Park may be the best place in the state to witness this transition.

By November, the dazzling fall foliage of the maple and sweetgum trees reaches its peak and offers a pleasant respite from whatever troubles you. The short hike around Lake Daingerfield is one of the most beautiful in the state and a great opportunity for quiet meditation.

The park also offers excellent picnicking, fishing, swimming, and a number of potluck Dutch oven events throughout the year. The park accommodations include fifty-eight campsites with standard amenities and three Civilian Conservation Corps–built vintage cabins.

455 Park Rd. 17
Daingerfield, TX 75638
(903) 645-2921
www.tpwd.texas.gov/state-parks/daingerfield

INTREPID TEXAN

In a state where football is king, no one ever earned a crown as impressively as the Daingerfield Tigers in 1983. The current holder of the national record for most shutouts in a season, they are considered the most dominant team in Texas history and rank second only to the 1969 Texas Longhorns national championship squad on the list of the most memorable Texas teams at the professional, college, or high school level.

PEDAL THROUGH A RAILROAD TUNNEL

The Caprock Canyons Trailway extends sixty-four miles along abandoned railway beds and runs through three separate Panhandle counties. Opened in 1993, it features more than fifty bridges and a thrilling pass through the 742-foot Clarity Tunnel, an old railroad passage through the Caprock.

The Caprock Canyons State Park is an excellent locale for hikes, mountain bikes, and horse rides but also offers compelling lessons in geology. The paved road in exposes visitors to 250 million years of geological formation punctuated by white streaks that cap the layer of each era. Paleo Indians hunted the ancestors of modern bison here ten thousand years ago, and the 15,314-acre spread is currently home to the official state bison herd. The herd is populated by descendants of Charles and Mary Ann Goodnight's successful 1878 attempt to save the species, which had dwindled from more than thirty million head to only a thousand when the Goodnights commenced the effort.

850 Caprock Canyon Park Rd.
Quitaque, TX 79255
(806) 455-1492
www.tpwd.texas.gov/state-parks/caprock-canyons

INTREPID TEXAN

One of the most picturesque waterfalls and some of the most impressive canyon features in the state are located in the Caprock region, near Silverton. The Linguish Falls and the Narrows (also referred to as the Linguish Narrows) lie on private land in an area sometimes referred to as Los Lingos Canyon. A blue norther killed three unprepared Texas Tech campers here in 1960.

DEBATE THE EZEKIEL FLYING MACHINE

Despite incessant license plate proclamation, North Carolina was not "First in Flight."

Sure, on December 17, 1903, at Kitty Hawk, the Wright Flyer became the first powered, heavier-than-air machine to achieve *controlled*, sustained flight. A year earlier, however, Reverend Burrell Cannon's Ezekiel Airship was the first powered, heavier-than-air machine to achieve sustained flight—the pilot just couldn't control it.

In 1900, Cannon came to believe he'd been called by God to build a flying machine. He'd studied the Book of Ezekiel and was fascinated by the description of an "aircraft" powered by "a wheel in the middle of a wheel" that lifted creatures up from the earth. By 1902, he completed a twenty-six-foot flying machine constructed of a light metal frame, an almost circular, fabric-covered flying wing, and two pairs of wheels below the wing. The outer wheels were designed to taxi the craft up to takeoff velocity, and the inner wheels were paddle operated, devised to drive the craft once it was aloft. On the maiden voyage, it flew 167 feet and clipped a fence post.

The Northeast Texas Rural Heritage Depot and Museum has a life-size replica of the original craft, which was destroyed while en route to the 1904 St. Louis World's Fair.

200 W. Marshall St.
Pittsburg, TX
(903) 946-3243

SEE THE HUECO TANKS

The Hueco Tanks are a unique rock formation in the desert just northeast of El Paso. The "tanks" are actually hollows in the rocks that catch and hold rainwater, which makes them particularly indispensable for the animals who make the dry region their home. The site has been important to Native Americans in the area for more than ten thousand years, and the hike, which is fairly moderate, allows you to view some of the five thousand pictographs they etched onto the rocks.

An excellent destination for rock climbing and bouldering as well, the park is never crowded and the tanks are a great way to spend some time away from El Paso or the Guadalupe Mountains (ninety miles east on U.S. Hwy. 62). Camping sites are available inside the 860-acre park if you want to make a day of it.

Hueco Tanks State Historic Site
6900 Hueco Tanks Rd. No. 1
El Paso, TX 79938
(915) 857-1135
www.tpwd.texas.gov/state-parks/hueco-tanks

ENDURE
THE HOTTER THAN HELL 100

One of the oldest, largest, and least hospitable cycling events in the world, the Hotter Than Hell 100 is a Texas-sized dare, pitting wild-eyed fitness junkies against the sweltering heat of a North Texas summer. In 1982, the Wichita Falls Bicycle Club chipped in with a crazy idea to promote their town's centennial celebration: a hundred miles in hundred-degree weather. Today, as the event's web page notes, it's a "Texas 'Ride' of Passage."

Held annually on the last Saturday in August, the Hotter Than Hell 100 attracts more than ten thousand riders a year. The event begins at 7:05 a.m., and, as a precautionary measure, prospective hundred-mile riders must reach the sixty-mile mark no later than 12:30 p.m. If they don't make it, they do not qualify to finish the hundred-mile segment and settle for the completion of a shorter route. Most participants finish the course in six to nine hours.

www.hh100.org

INTREPID TEXAN

If you have some extra time to spend in the Wichita Falls area, the wildly underappreciated, 1899-acre Copper Breaks State Park is a little over ninety miles west on U.S. Hwy. 287. Featuring two small lakes and ten miles of hiking trails, it's nice and quiet and well off the beaten path.

www.tpwd.texas.gov/state-parks/copper-breaks

BASK IN THE SUN
AT SOUTH PADRE ISLAND

The spring break capital of Texas and one of the most popular spring break destinations in the United States, South Padre Island is arguably a better place to visit before or after March when the college crowds recede and prices drop and especially if you're looking for some peace and quiet.

South Padre Island was separated from the Padre Island National Seashore by the installation of the Mansfield Channel in 1964, and the first five miles or so north from the Queen Isabella Causeway offer accomodations in line with most modern beach resort meccas. The next twenty-nine miles of the beach are more primitive.

At the base of the causeway, the Port Isabel Lighthouse is the only lighthouse in Texas that offers public access. Out in the Gulf itself, the number of watersports seem to increase every year. If the sun and sand are not enough, windsurfing, kiteboarding, kayaking, fishing, surf-fishing, or skydiving are all viable options.

www.sopadre.com

TRY THE TEXAS WATER SAFARI

Even though the Texas Water Safari has been around longer, it's something of a bookend event to the more widely known Hotter Than Hell 100. Held annually the second Saturday in June since 1963, the Safari is a 262-mile canoe race that begins in San Marcos and ends at Seadrift on the Gulf Coast after clearing the Guadalupe River and crossing San Antonio Bay. Participants must transport all the gear they need with them, receiving only water, ice, and medical supplies along the way. They have one hundred hours to complete the course, and possible complications and obstructions include dams, logjams, downed trees, alligators, water moccasins, mosquitos, fire ants, and sharks. There are twelve preestablished checkpoints, including the finish line. The fastest recorded team time is 29:46. The fastest recorded solo time is 36:03.

www.texaswatersafari.org

HISTORY AND CULTURE

GET A GLIMPSE OF THE PLEISTOCENE AGE
AT THE MAMMOTH NATIONAL MONUMENT

The Mammoth National Monument in Waco is the scene of an ice age mishap.

Approximately sixty-seven thousand years ago, a nursery herd of mammoths (six adult females and ten juveniles) died during a flash flood near the confluence of the Brazos and Bosque Rivers. They were buried in the mud, and then, 65,022 years later, two teenagers stumbled onto some of their bones while hunting for arrowheads. The rest, they say, is history. Or a fascinating glimpse into prehistory.

In July 2014, the resultant dig site became a national monument. It features a short, paved stroll and a climate-controlled viewing center, where the fossils can be observed in the arrangement they were discovered in.

Located just a few miles off Interstate 35, this remarkable find is a must-do in Central Texas.

6220 Steinbeck Bend Dr.
Waco, TX 76708
www.nps.gov/waco/index.htm

INTREPID TEXAN

Sports fans may also enjoy stopping off at
the Texas Sports Hall of Fame, just fifteen
minutes away at 1108 S. University Parks Dr.

www.tshof.org

TAKE IN THE ODESSA METEOR CRATER

In 1892, twelve-year-old Julius D. Henderson rode his horse out in search of a lost calf. He located the wandering bovine grazing in an odd, oblong-shaped drop-off in the landscape and told his parents about it when he returned home.

In 1920, Elisha Virgil Graham discovered a peculiar, lava-like rock near the center of the sunken area. Graham gave the rock to his friend Samuel R. McKinney, the first mayor of Odessa. McKinney fancied the strange rock and used it as a paperweight in his office.

In 1922, A. B. Bibbins, a Baltimore geologist visiting the mayor's office on business, noticed the peculiar rock and examined it more closely. Bibbins declared that the paperweight was actually a meteorite, and McKinney permitted him to dislodge a shard and send it to George P. Merrill, the head curator of the Department of Geology at the United States National Museum (now the National Museum of Natural History at the Smithsonian Institution), for analysis. Merrill confirmed Bibbins's conclusion: the paperweight was a meteorite composed of extremely hard nickel-iron.

The Odessa Meteor Crater became the second officially designated meteorite crater on Earth and was designated a National Natural Landmark on October 24, 1965.

Odessa Meteor Crater and Museum
3100 Meteor Crater Rd.
Odessa, TX 79764
(432) 381-0946

DISCOVER
THE ALIBATES FLINT QUARRIES NATIONAL MONUMENT

When the Great Lakes began forming around fourteen thousand years ago (at the end of the last glacial period), the indigenous peoples that hunted mammoths in the Great Plains were already using flint in weapons and tools from what we now call the Alibates Flint Quarries. High-quality arrowheads and spearheads were integral to human survival, and the durable, rainbow-hued flint from this site (just north of Amarillo) was widely sought after and traded across the region.

The Alibates Flint Quarries were the first national monument in Texas, and park personnel today offer fascinating short hikes and seasonal programs.

Cas Johnson Rd.
Fritch, TX 79036
(806) 857-6680
www.nps.gov/alfl/index.htm

INTREPID TEXAN
Southeast of Perryton the remains of an ancient indigenous community referred to as "the Buried City" sits virtually unknown to most Texans. Tours are available through the Courson Archaeological Research Group. www.coursonarchresearch.com

EXAMINE
THE ANCIENT NATIVE AMERICAN PETROGLYPHS AT SEMINOLE CANYON

Humans began inhabiting the Seminole Canyon region ten to twelve thousand years ago and creating art on cave and shelter walls about five thousand years later, continuing to add to their stone canvases until about two thousand years ago. The renderings on the Fate Bell Shelter walls in particular are believed to be some of the oldest in North America.

Located about forty-five miles west of Del Rio and just east of the impressive Pecos River High Bridge, the 2,173-acre Seminole Canyon State Park gets its name from the Black Seminole scouts who served in the region during the mid- to late nineteenth century. Today, this fascinating destination offers several campsites with basic amenities, guided tours of the Fate Bell Shelter, and other intriguing sights and hikes. Once there, you can also get information regarding the nearby Amistad National Recreation Area boat tours, which allow folks to see the magnificent pictograph sites at the Panther and Parida caves.

U.S. Highway 90
Comstock, TX 78837
(432) 292-4464
www.tpwd.texas.gov/state-parks/seminole-canyon

WALK AROUND
THE CADDO MOUNDS

The mythical expanse of Texas is difficult for many folks (including most Texans) to get their heads around, and most perceptions are based on the state since the Spanish laid claim to it in 1519. It's mind-boggling to think there could be more to Texas, but there is, and one of the best places to experience this revelation is at the Caddo Mounds State Historic Site. Located about twenty-five miles west of Nacogdoches, the 397-acre park is the only preserve of Caddo mounds in the state and features evidence of occupation for more than twelve thousand years. A Southern Caddo Indian culture known as the Hasinai flourished in the area from around A.D. 800 to about 1300.

Unlike their hunter-gatherer precedents, the Hasinai arrived with highly developed horticultural methods and a fixed, complex culture. Their success and productivity fostered trade networks (stretching from the Gulf Coast to the Great Lakes), advanced social and political hierarchies, and large ceremonial centers. All that's left of the Hasinai at the site are three burial mounds and the remains of a borrow pit, which was a human-made depression created during construction of the mounds.

Before six European, Mexican, Texan, and U.S. flags flew over Texas, the Caddo thrived for almost five hundred years, masters of agriculture, diplomacy, and early architecture in the region. They created magnificent ceremonial blades and effigies and crafted some of the finest aboriginal ceramics on American soil, but their most famous contribution regards our nomenclature. The Hasinai called the first Spanish explorers they encountered "tayshas," meaning allies and friends. The Spanish later pronounced the word "tejas" and referred to the area as the Kingdom of Tejas.

1649 TX-21
Alto, TX 75925
(936) 858-3218
www.thc.texas.gov/historic-sites/caddo-mounds-state-historic-site

---

INTREPID TEXAN

A great place to stay when you visit the Caddo Mounds is the beautiful 660-acre Mission Tejas State Park, just seven miles west on State Hwy. 21.

www.tpwd.texas.gov/state-parks/mission-tejas

VISIT THE ALAMO

The Alamo is a Texas and American icon harking back to a spirit of defiance that was prevalent across the Western frontier throughout the nineteenth century, and it has become the symbol for those who chose death over defeat midway through the war for Texas independence.

Originally known as the Mission San Antonio de Valero, the site was founded in 1718 by the Spanish to serve as a midway point between northern Mexico and the missions in what would become East Texas. Though dwarfed by taller buildings around it, the 4.2-acre complex and the fifty-foot cenotaph that lists the names of the defenders who died in the Battle of the Alamo receive more than 2.5 million visitors a year. The site provides Texans, history buffs, and international fans a practical, spatial context for the legendary standoff, and few leave uninspired.

300 Alamo Plaza
San Antonio, TX 78205
(210) 225-1391
www.thealamo.org

EXPERIENCE
THE FORT WORTH STOCKYARDS

The Stockyards National Historic District in Fort Worth is one of the most popular tourist destinations in Texas. Folks come from all over the world to get a glimpse of the Old West, and the Stockyards capably oblige. Local cowboys drive Texas longhorn cattle through the red brick streets every day at 11:30 a.m. and 4:00 p.m. The world's largest honky-tonk, Billy Bob's Texas, is open every night, and the Stockyards Championship Rodeo is staged every weekend (at 8:00 p.m. on Friday and Saturday). The intervals can be filled with visits to any number of historic buildings, bars, restaurants, shops, and other attractions, including the Texas Cowboy Hall of Fame, the Stockyards Museum, the White Elephant Saloon, and M. L. Leddy's, which has been crafting handmade boots, saddles, belts, and buckles since 1922.

INTREPID TEXAN
The National Cowgirl Museum and Hall of Fame is also located in Fort Worth, about ten minutes away from the Stockyards (at 720 Gendy St.).

WONDER
AT THE JOHNSON SPACE CENTER

Located twenty-five miles southeast of Houston on Interstate 45, the 1,600-acre Johnson Space Center is the official headquarters and training base for American astronauts, the site of Mission Control for the International Space Station, and home of the Orion Program, which is currently sorting out the logistics of deep space flight for future missions to Mars and other space-related endeavors. For almost four decades, every NASA astronaut and any space explorer from partner nations who has spent time at the International Space Station or been part of a space shuttle team has received his or her training at the Johnson Space Center. The importance of this facility can't be overstated, and ninety-minute tram tours, which include an Astronaut Training Facility Tour and a Mission Control Center Tour, are offered seven days a week.

INTREPID TEXAN
Make sure you visit Building 9. It houses the Space Vehicle Mockup Facility and a next-generation humanoid Valkyrie robot project known as the R5.

CONRAD

NASA

A veteran of two Gemini flights, Charles "Pete" Conrad was Mission Commander for the November 1969 Apollo 12 expedition. A native Philadelphian and a Princeton graduate, Conrad followed Armstrong and Aldrin and became the third man to walk on the Moon. Traveling aboard the Lunar Module Intrepid—Conrad and Lunar Module Pilot Alan Bean landed on the Moon at the Ocean of Storms, just a few feet away from the unmanned Surveyor 3 spacecraft that had nestled down onto the lunar surface two and a half years earlier. The Apollo 12 Moon landing was an extremely challenging maneuver and was considered one of the most precise landings in the history of navigation.

Once Conrad planted his feet on the Moon, he loped around in high spirits as he became accustomed to the lunar gravity. A flurry of Moon dust made their work difficult as Conrad and Bean set up the Apollo Lunar Surface Experiment Package (ALSEP) during their first extravehicular activity which lasted approximately four hours.

Once the ALSEP started operating, Conrad and Bean began the exciting work of Moon rock collecting. Conrad described one sample as "a pure piece of glass," and after a second Moon walk, the two astronauts collected a total of about 75 pounds of material. Apollo 12 did not have the worldwide attention of Apollo 11's first Moon landing, but it proved that venturing to this new world would happen again, and that even more exciting explorations of space were on the horizon.

SEE THE TEXAS STATE CAPITOL

When the Texas State Capitol was completed in 1888, it was the seventh-largest building in the world and stood seven feet taller than its national counterpart in Washington, D.C. Transporting the pink granite alone (donated by the owners of Granite Mountain in Marble Falls) that was necessary to construct the exterior required fifteen thousand railroad cars, and the interior woodwork was crafted from several linear miles of the highest quality mahogany, walnut, ash, cedar, pine, and oak in the region. The terrazzo-floored capitol rotunda displays paintings and sculptures of noteworthy Lone Star leaders, and a $75 million underground extension was completed in 1993.

Tours of the capitol are available every day, and events such as the annual Texas Book Festival are actually held on the surrounding grounds.

1100 Congress Ave.
Austin, TX 78701
www.tspb.texas.gov/prop/tc/tc/capitol.html

INTREPID TEXAN
Just east of the capitol, the Texas State Library and Archives Commission is an incredible resource for general cultural and historical research. www.tsl.texas.gov

---

INSPECT
THE SIXTH FLOOR MUSEUM

On November 22, 1963, Texas became the site of one of the darkest acts in American history. John F. Kennedy, the thirty-fifth president of the United States, was assassinated in broad daylight as he rode in a presidential motorcade through Dallas. The crime has never been satisfactorily investigated, explained, or put to rest, and this brazen act traumatized the nation in ways we still don't fully understand. The Kennedy assassination essentially eclipses almost everything else that Dallas, the ninth-largest city in the United States, has to offer. Half a million folks visit the Sixth Floor Museum and the grassy knoll every year, trying to make sense of it. The museum offers viewings of the Zapruder film, oral histories, a Jack Ruby collection, and special exhibits.

411 Elm St.
Dallas, TX 75202
(214) 747-6660
www.jfk.org

INTREPID TEXAN
The grave of Lee Harvey Oswald, the misguided crank who JFK's assassination was officially and solely pinned on, is thirty minutes away in Fort Worth's Shannon Rose Hill Memorial Park cemetery.

General store in downtown Jefferson (page 28)

View from the South Rim at Big Bend National Park (page 40)

Jacob's Well in Wimberley (page 48)

Historic lighthouse at Port Isabel (page 64)

Enchanted Rock near Fredericksburg (page 50)

San Fransisco de la Espada at sunrise (page 2)

Steel spire at the top of Guadalupe Peak (page 162)

Padre Island National Seashore (page 44)

Buddy Holly Statue in Lubbock (page 166)

Abandoned Contrabando movie set piece on River Road (page 142)

Boots on a fence outside Marfa (page 4)

Dreadnought battleship, the USS *Texas*

VISIT
THE SAN JACINTO BATTLEGROUND STATE HISTORIC SITE

At first mention, it could be argued that this stop is a formality attraction. Yes, Sam Houston and the Texian fighters defeated Santa Anna here on April 21, 1836, but the battlefield itself is just a green space without compelling particulars, and the most notable aspect of the 567-foot San Jacinto Monument, which stands alongside the Houston Ship Channel, is that it's almost thirteen feet taller than the Washington Monument.

The real star of the complex is the state historic site's museum ship, the USS *Texas* (BB-35). Also referred to as "Battleship Texas," the USS *Texas* was the first American battleship to be declared a National Historic Landmark, the first American battleship to be converted into a museum ship, the only surviving World War I–era dreadnought battleship, and one of the only remaining ships that served in both world wars. Seeing the USS *Texas* from the 489-foot observation floor of the San Jacinto Monument (reached by elevator) is interesting, but boarding the vessel itself and exploring the main and lower decks is mind-blowing. The historical context, the practical details, the cramped bunks, the gun stations—it's imagination-provoking, riveting stuff.

3523 Independence Pkwy.
La Porte, TX 77571
(281) 479-2431
www.tpwd.texas.gov/state-parks/san-jacinto-battleground

LEARN MORE ABOUT BUFFALO SOLDIERS
AT FORT DAVIS

The indigenous peoples of Texas were a fierce lot, so it probably wouldn't be fair to say that they feared any enemy, but they had a healthy respect for a new warrior that appeared in Fort Davis in 1867.

Known as one half of the Ninth U.S. Cavalry to their American military brass, their Native American foes called them "Buffalo Soldiers" because of their coarse, curly hair and ferocity in battle. These African American troops manned the last fights against the Apache in Texas and were then transferred to the Arizona Territory, where they helped subdue Geronimo.

The 523-acre Fort Davis National Historic Site is a good place to familiarize yourself with how the Buffalo Soldiers lived and fought. It is also one of the best preserved examples of a frontier military outpost in the Southwest.

101 Lt. Flipper Dr., #1379
Fort Davis, TX 79734
(432) 426-3224
www.nps.gov/foda/index.htm

INTREPID TEXAN

The Davis Mountains State Park right up
State Hwy. 118 is home to the outstanding
adobe-style Indian Lodge hotel and eight
dozen great mile-high camping spots. It is
also close to the McDonald Observatory
and the town of Fort Davis.

WATCH A SIX-MAN FOOTBALL GAME

Football is now a religion in Texas.

Gridiron megachurches come replete with the finest indoor practice facilities, the most expensive artificially turfed fields, and the biggest, brightest jumbotrons—even high schools are spending $80 million on "worship" venues. The problem, of course, is that football in Texas is no longer just a game, pitting town against town. The big championship programs at the high school level sit mostly in wealthy suburbs, and the boosters there already solicit and recruit the top athletes (and their parents) from underfunded junior high schools in the inner cities.

There are still some places, however, where a game with real hometown athletes and real hometown fans continues to hold sway. The sport at the six-man level, for example, always requires all hands on deck, freshman through senior. The 2017 six-man state championship team from Strawn even featured a female place-kicker.

SOME SIX-MAN FOOTBALL VENUES

Coyote Field

Richland Springs High School
700 W. Coyote Trail
Richland Springs, TX 76871

Wilkerson Field

Calvert High School
310 Hickory St.
Calvert, TX 77837

Cougar Stadium

Aquilla High School
404 N. Richards
Aquilla, TX 76622

Dick Todd Field

Crowell High School
400 E. Logan St.
Crowell, TX 79227

Coyote Den

Borden County High School
240 W. Kincaid St.
Gail, TX 79738

PONDER THE HANGING TREE
IN GOLIAD

The most appealing thing about the courthouse square in Goliad is the beautiful, massive oak tree that stands on the north lawn of the grounds, especially if you don't know the tree's history.

For several years, trials were held under the oak tree itself, and guilty verdicts that mandated death sentences were carried out in minutes, as soon as the guilty could be noosed and hanged from a sturdy branch. The tree was also enlisted by lynching parties during the infamous Cart War of 1857, when Anglo-American wagon haulers grew frustrated over having to compete with the cheaper Mexican American oxcart haulers for freight being shipped out of Indianola. Disgruntled Anglos began destroying their competitors' oxcarts, stealing their freight, and, in many cases, taking their lives. The massive oak tree was the site of an untold number of summary executions until the sitting governor began sending Texas Rangers to escort the Mexican American haulers.

Courthouse Square
Goliad, TX

TRACE THE FOOTSTEPS
OF DOC HOLLIDAY AND WYATT EARP AT FORT GRIFFIN

Fans of the Old West could hardly do better than a stop at the Fort Griffin State Historic Site in Shackelford County. Fort Griffin sat on a hill just north of present-day Albany, and the settlement that sprang up at the base of the hill became known as the "Babylon of the West." Legendary lawman Wyatt Earp met Doc Holliday there, and they became fast friends. The community bustled with cowboys, gunfighters, gamblers, buffalo hunters, and "painted ladies"—including John Wesley Hardin, John Selman, Lottie Deno, and Big Nose Kate. From 1874 to 1878, Fort Griffin was the largest city between Dallas and El Paso and an important station on the Great Western Trail.

Today, there isn't much left, but what is there is picturesque and easy to peruse. The park office even offers complimentary golf carts to tour the hill. History buffs can spend a whole day here, examining the sites of the Bush Knob Massacre, the Butterfield Stage Clear Fork Station, Daws Crossing, and the intersection of the aforementioned Great Western Trail and the Goodnight-Loving Trail. The state historic site is also the home of the official state longhorn herd.

1701 N. U.S. Hwy. 283
Albany, TX 76430
(325) 762-3592
www.thc.texas.gov/historic-sites/fort-griffin-state-historic-site

MARVEL
AT THE IMMACULATE CONCEPTION
CATHEDRAL

Dedicated in July 1856, the Gothic revival–style Immaculate Conception Cathedral in Brownsville is still composed of 250,000 of the original handmade bricks and retains twenty-nine original stained-glass windows majestically depicting dramatic scenes from the Bible (ranging from the namesake Immaculate Conception to Jesus being taken down from the cross). It also still has the original wooden pews, which comfortably seat almost four hundred.

Its magnificent chandeliers, which hang from the vaulted, blue nave ceilings, were shipped over from France in 1865, and it is home to an antique pipe organ that arrived in 1935.

Listed in the National Register of Historic Places in 1980, the Immaculate Conception Cathedral is a stunning monument to the Catholic faith and the miracle the cathedral is named for.

1218 E. Jefferson St.
Brownsville, TX 78520
(956) 546-3178
www.immaculateconceptioncathedral.org

EXPLORE GUSHERS
AT THE EAST TEXAS OIL MUSEUM

Way before HBO's *Westworld* there was "Eastworld" at the East Texas Oil Museum. Located on the campus of Kilgore College, the facility features a life-size indoor replica of a 1930s boomtown, complete with primitive human automatons in vintage automobiles and trucks and a horse-drawn carriage, all stuck in the mud. The museum also includes life-size models of a general store, machine shop, barber shop, post office, drug store, gas station, cinema, and an "Elevator Ride to the Center of the Earth." The animated residents haunt the place, especially the barber.

To date, the East Texas Oil Field has produced six billion barrels of oil and, at the height of the oil boom, over 1,100 producing wooden oil derricks sat inside the Kilgore city limits. Oil production has obviously slowed down, but the Kilgore boomtown lives on.

1201 S. Henderson Blvd.
Kilgore, TX 75662
(903) 983-8295

FENCE YOURSELF IN
AT THE DEVIL'S ROPE MUSEUM

When barbed wire (the Devil's Rope) was first introduced by big ranchers in Texas in 1875, Texans weren't having it. Cattle drives required access to public land and public water sources, and rank-and-file Texans despised fencing off the frontier. They began sneaking out at night and cutting down miles of barbed wire fencing as fast at the big ranches put it up. It led to what became known as the Fence-Cutter's War, where the big ranches hired private security and poached Texas Rangers from the state to police the fence lines of their property. In the end, the frontier, the cattle drivers, and, arguably, true Texans lost. Hence the devilish moniker.

The Devil's Rope Museum showcases every variety of barbed wire, including "entanglement" wires from modern American wars.

100 Kingsley St.
McLean, TX 79057
(806) 779-2225
www.barbwiremuseum.com

INTREPID TEXAN
The abandoned old Dixie Motel and Restaurant sits a few minutes east on First Street. Its fortunes faded when Interstate 40 replaced historic Route 66.

JAM WITH JANIS
AT THE MUSEUM OF THE GULF COAST

Housed in a former bank building, a section of the Museum of the Gulf Coast is devoted to Port Arthur's most famous native, 1960s rock icon Janis Joplin. A misfit in her hometown and the subject of no small amount of scorn and ridicule at the University of Texas, Joplin moved to California and became a superstar in the music world, belting out psychedelic blues and gut-wrenching soul as powerfully as few artists before or since have even attempted much less achieved. Her exhibit includes photos, memorabilia, and a full-size replica of the Queen of Rock and Roll's 1965 Porsche. Originally oyster-shell white, Joplin had one of her roadies spruce the vehicle up, covering it with dreamlike landscapes, flowing waterways, a butterfly, and a symbolic eye. The original vehicle fetched $1.76 million at Sotheby's in 2016.

The museum is home to three Halls of Fame. The music hall recognizes local-born talents, such as Clarence "Gatemouth" Brown, Edgar Winter, and George Jones. The sports hall celebrates the accomplishments of area legends, such as Babe Didrikson Zaharias and former Dallas Cowboys head coach Jimmy Johnson.

The facility also includes works of the influential native painter and graphic artist Robert Rauschenberg.

700 Procter St.
Port Arthur, TX 77640
(409) 982-7000
www.museumofthegulfcoast.org/janis-joplin

LEARN THE TRUTH
ABOUT THE TRUER DER UNION MONUMENT

In 1862, the Confederate States of America declared martial law in Central Texas, due to significant resistance to the Civil War. Jacob Kuechler, a surveyor of German descent and conscientious objector to the war, agreed to serve as a guide for sixty-one other conscientious objectors (mostly German) attempting to escape the reach of Confederate conscription by fleeing to Mexico. Confederate irregulars caught them at the Nueces River and killed thirty-four, taking the rest prisoner.

On August 10, 1866, a 20-foot obelisk, funded by donations from local residents and families of the victims, was dedicated in Comfort, Texas. The main structure weighs 35,700 pounds and includes four tablets listing the victims' names. A thirty-six-star American flag—representing the number of states in the Union at the time of the dedication—flies over the site.

High Street, between Third and Fourth
Comfort, TX 78013

INTREPID TEXAN
A large percentage of the immigrants who settled the Comfort area were known as *Freidenkers* or "freethinkers." The Comfort freethinkers were irreligious and advocated reason and democracy over religious and political authoritarianism. The community didn't have a church for the first forty years of its existence.

REMEMBER THE AUTHOR
OF THE GREAT SOCIETY

The Vietnam War ruined the broader legacy of the thirty-sixth president of the United States, Lyndon Baines Johnson. This is arguably unfortunate because his legislative accomplishments are unparalleled in modern history.

During LBJ's sixty-three-month term in office, he signed four civil rights acts, four environmental protections acts, three wilderness protection acts, three transportation acts, two higher education acts, two economic opportunity acts, two food protection acts, one Endangered Species Act, one Historic Preservation Act, a National Foundation on the Arts and Humanities Act (which created the National Endowment for the Arts and the National Endowment for the Humanities), a Public Broadcasting Act (which led to the creation of National Public Radio), a Bilingual Education Act, a Truth in Lending Act, the first Cigarette Labeling and Advertising Act (mandating health warnings), and a Social Security Act that authorized Medicare. Love him or hate him or both, LBJ's aggressive flurry of domestic programs was enacted to foster a "Great Society" for all, and he remains the boldest, most productive political leader Texas has ever produced. The 1,571-acre Lyndon B. Johnson National Historical Park in Stonewall is a great place to consider his legacy.

199 Park Rd. 52
Stonewall, TX 78671
www.tpwd.texas.gov/state-parks/lyndon-b-johnson

● ●

VISIT
THE BRISCOE WESTERN ART MUSEUM

San Antonio is a great place for remembering that there are at least two sides to every story in Texas, and a wonderful spot to start is the outdoor McNutt Sculpture Garden at the Briscoe Western Art Museum. The sculptures devoted to Texas's indigenous cultures, including Denny Haskew's *Strength of the Maker*, R. V. Greeves's *Bird Woman,* and John Coleman's *Rainmaker*, are striking and beautiful. Equally compelling are Kiko Guerra's *El Caporal* and Bill Nebeker's *The Eyes of Texas*. And the interior space features several unexpected artifacts, including Santa Anna's sword and Pancho Villa's saddle.

210 W. Market St.
San Antonio, TX 78205
(210) 299-4499
www.briscoemuseum.org

INTREPID TEXAN
The Texas Air Museum at Stinson Municipal Airport is worth a visit. San Antonio is considered the birthplace of U.S. military aviation, and the two barn-burning Stinson sisters, Katherine and Marjorie, trained dozens of American and Canadian men to fly combat missions in World War I—but weren't allowed to join the fight themselves.

PAY YOUR RESPECTS
AT MONUMENT HILL

Lots of folks today—including too many Texans—forget that our troubles with Santa Anna didn't end after his defeat at the hands of Sam Houston on April 21, 1836, or even after he signed the Treaty of Velasco, which recognized Texas independence a few weeks later. In 1842, Santa Anna (who had regained the Mexican presidency a year earlier) began encouraging his military to begin raids into Texas to destabilize the young nation and discourage foreign investment. San Antonio was seized by Mexican troops twice in 1842, and during the second go-round, Texans responded with force. Though the confrontations led to Mexican withdrawal, three dozen Texans perished at Dawson's Creek, and several more died during the ill-fated Mier Expedition. In 1848, their remains were collected and interred in a common tomb in a sandstone vault at what is now known as the Monument Hill State Historic Site, which shares its seven-acre location with the Kreische Brewery State Historic Site.

As part of the Texas Centennial celebrations in 1936, a forty-eight-foot monument adorned with an Art Deco mural was placed to mark the grave. Besides being a great place to learn the whole story and pay your respects, Monument Hill also offers nice hikes and impressive views of the Colorado River.

414 TX-92 Spur
La Grange, TX 78945
www.tpwd.texas.gov/state-parks/monument-hill-kreische-brewery

RETURN TO TEXAS
AT GREENWOOD CEMETERY

Texas literary giant Larry McMurtry borrowed a substantial portion of the plotline for *Lonesome Dove* from the life of Oliver Loving, a longtime partner of Charles Goodnight. Loving established the Goodnight-Loving Trail with Charles, and they participated in several cattle ventures together. On their last drive, Loving and a scout went ahead of the herd to negotiate a contract but were attacked by Native Americans. Loving was injured but made it to Fort Sumner, where he died of gangrene.

Goodnight had promised Loving that his remains would be returned to Texas if he died outside the state and, after temporary interment at Fort Sumner (while Goodnight got the herd to Colorado), Loving's body was exhumed and returned to Texas, where it was reburied at Greenwood Cemetery in Weatherford.

Black cowboy Bose Ikard, the man *Lonesome Dove*'s Joshua Deets is based on, is also buried at Greenwood Cemetery.

Located behind the Parker County Jail in Weatherford,
just off Fort Worth Highway.

CHANGE HISTORY
AT AVENGER FIELD

The barnstorming Stinson sisters in San Antonio trained male pilots to fly in World War I but were prohibited from joining the fray. Beginning in November 1942, more than a thousand women were trained to fly in World War II and transferred to Avenger Field. As part of the Women's Auxiliary Ferrying Squadron and Women's Flying Training Detachment (WASP), female pilots flew every aircraft in the army's arsenal, towing gunnery targets, transporting equipment, and flight-testing repaired aircraft to make sure they were airworthy. The WASP flyers served at more than 120 bases around the country and suffered thirty-seven casualties in the line of duty. In June 1944, Army Air Forces commanding general Henry "Hap" Arnold sought to officially designate the WASP pilots members of the United States military, but the U.S. Congress declined his request. After a lengthy battle with their own government, the WASP aviatrices were granted military status in 1977.

The National WASP WWII Museum in Sweetwater features some of the actual aircraft the WASP pilots flew, photographs, memorabilia, and oral histories. It is the best place in the country to learn about WASP history.

210 Avenger Field Rd.
Sweetwater, TX 79556
(325) 235-0099
www.waspmuseum.org/index.html

INVESTIGATE
THE TEXAS RANGER HALL OF FAME
AND MUSEUM

There's not a more iconic American law enforcement institution than the legendary Texas Rangers. Most of us were first introduced to them in the television series *The Lone Ranger*, which ran from 1949 to 1957, and children were still watching the serial well into the 1970s. Since 1910, almost four hundred American movies have featured a Texas Ranger as a main character, and recent memory immediately conjures up such critically acclaimed classics as *No Country for Old Men* (2007), the remake of *True Grit* (2010), and *Hell or High Water* (2016).

Rangers retain statewide jurisdiction and have served as a policing arm and a paramilitary force in service of the Republic of Texas and the state of Texas. They have waged war, patrolled the border, provided security for the governor, broken up race riots, and ended the crime sprees of countless outlaws (including Sam Bass and Bonnie and Clyde). Historically speaking, they have always been a formidable force, usually for the good—but not always.

The Texas Ranger Hall of Fame and Museum is a great place to learn about their role and legacy in terms of Lone Star history.

100 Texas Ranger Trail
Waco, TX 76706
(254) 750-8631
www.texasranger.org

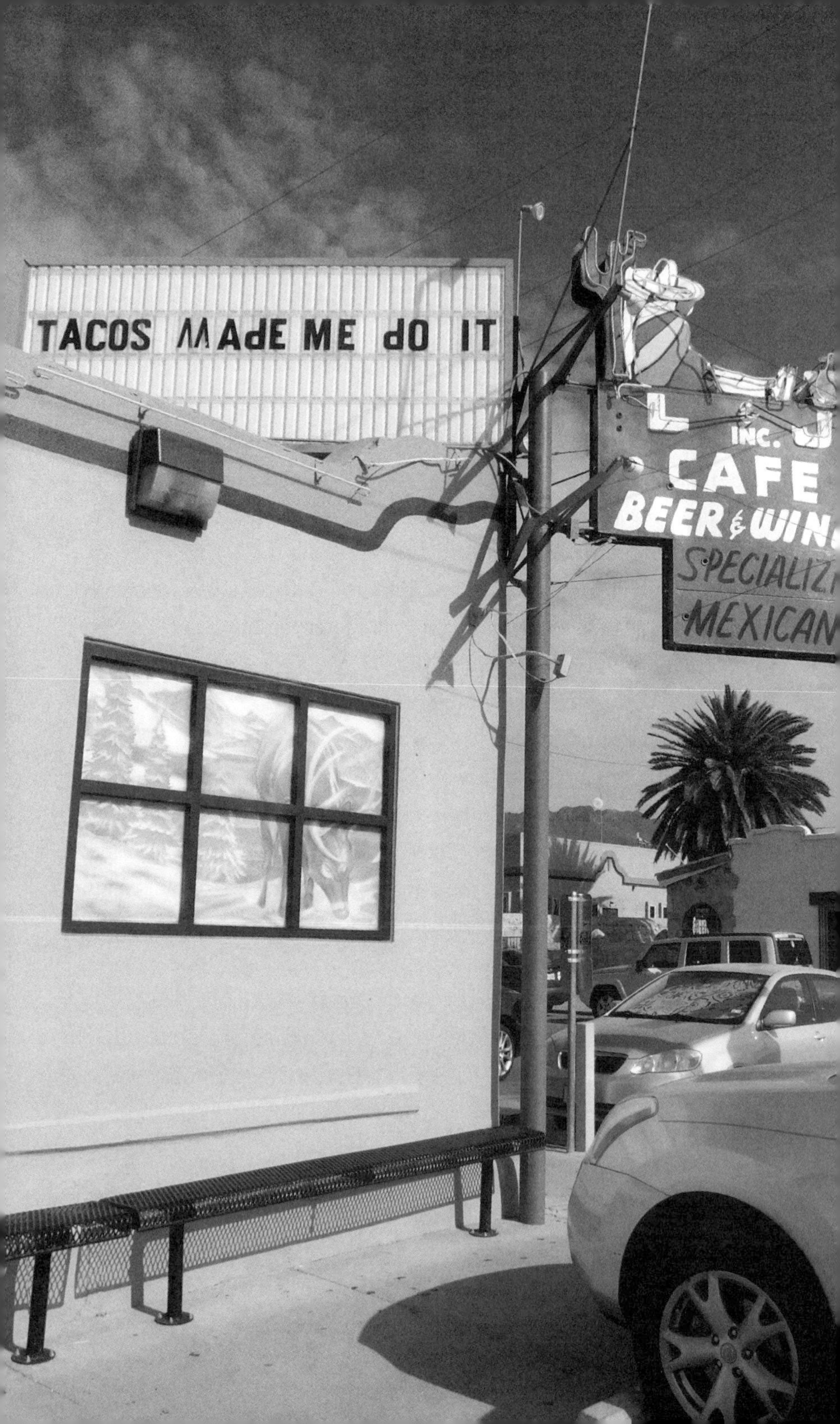
TACOS MAdE ME dO IT
INC.
CAFE
BEER & WIN
SPECIALIZ
MEXICAN

FOOD AND DRINK

EXPLORE
YOUR TEX-MEX ROOTS

The late eighteenth- and early nineteenth-century French gastronomic philosopher Jean Anthelme Brillat-Savarin once claimed that if you told him what you ate, he could tell you what you are. If Brillat-Savarin were diagnosing the diets of most Texans today, he might tell us we're Mexican. Or at least half-Mexican.

Yes, Mexicans prefer white cheese and corn tortillas, and Texans splurge on yellow cheese and choose flour tortillas and sometimes black beans, but there's more crossover than separation . . . and that's the way it should be. Tex-Mex is the perfect culinary embodiment of who Texans really are, embracing our minor differences and celebrating our major similarities. The kitchen truth of the matter sets us all free, and we celebrate it daily at breakfast, lunch, and dinner.

L&J Café (El Paso)
Located on the east side of El Paso; a go-to eatery right
next to the old graveyard and just off Interstate 10

3622 E. Missouri Ave.
El Paso, TX 79903
(915) 566-8418
www.landjcafe.com

Herbert's Taco Hut (San Marcos)
Located right off Interstate 35; a San Marcos and Texas
State University rugby favorite for thirty years

419 Riverside Dr.
San Marcos, TX 78666
(512) 392-2993

Matt's El Rancho (Austin)
Located on South Lamar; an Austin tradition since 1952

2613 S. Lamar Blvd.
Austin, TX 78704
(512) 462-9333
www.mattselrancho.com

Rio Grande Grill (Harlingen)
Es verdad. Smoked fish tacos and tasty
brisket under the same roof

417 W. Van Buren Ave.
Harlingen, TX 78550
(956) 423-1817
www.harlingenbbq.com

Garcia's Mexican Food (San Antonio)
Just breakfast and lunch but packs a punch

842 Fredericksburg Rd.
San Antonio, TX 78201
(210) 735-4525

EXPERIENCE
BBQ NIRVANA

"Barbecue may not be the road to world peace, but it's a start."

Thus spake the late, great Anthony Bourdain, the world's foremost ambassador for culinary exploration.

Here in Texas, the roads to BBQ may be paved, pea gravel, or red dirt, but they always arrive at an amicable space for a mealtime kum-ba-yah. The Dalai Lama of Texas BBQ is beef brisket, smoked till fall-apart tender and usually seasoned enough by wet or dry rubs and its own natural fats that sauce is optional. In fact, beef brisket is even moonlighting in tacos and nachos these days, subtly threatening a separation of church and state.

Beef ribs also offer enlightenment, and most pit masters will begrudgingly offer a pork, chicken, or sausage option and the occasional slab of smoked bologna. Potato salad, pinto beans, and a slice or two of white bread are the customary sides.

Cooper's Old Time Pit Bar-B-Que

Worth the detour to Llano, but the only
thing green on the menu is jalapenos

604 W. Young St.
Llano, TX 78643
(325) 247-5713
www.coopersbbq.com

Franklin Barbecue

An Austin favorite, but open for lunch only;
better get there four hours early

900 E. Eleventh St.
Austin, TX 78702
(512) 653-1187
www.franklinbbq.com

Heim Barbecue

Started as a food truck and still relatively new but
offers BBQ illumination in Cowtown; go early

1109 W. Magnolia Ave.
Fort Worth, TX 76104
(817) 882-6970
www.heimbbq.com

Church BBQ

Run by the New Zion Missionary Baptist Church in
Huntsville, the $12 all-you-can-eat deal is a revelation

2601 Montgomery Rd.
Huntsville, TX 77340
(936) 294-0884

City of Lockhart

Has three renowned BBQ joints: Black's Barbecue,
Kreuz Market, and Smitty's Market

EAT SOME CHICKEN-FRIED STEAK
(IT'S THE LAW)

In his 1968 meditation on the state of the state—*In a Narrow Grave: Essays on Texas*—Larry McMurtry put it plainly: "Only a rank degenerate would drive 1,500 miles across Texas without eating a chicken-fried steak."

He was right, of course, and one sunny day in May forty-three years later, the Texas State Legislature resolved that it be so in HR 1419. To wit (and paraphrased): "WHEREAS, Texans are renowned for their love of chicken fried steak, that exceptional dish that elevates the hearty flavor of beef to new heights by coating it in batter and breading and frying it until the ingredients are melded in a blissful union" and "WHEREAS, generations of Lone Star State residents have partaken of this beloved entrée" and "WHEREAS, this signature dish occupies a special place in the culinary culture of the Lone Star State, and Texas Chicken Fried Steak Day provides a welcome opportunity to pay homage to that shared legacy; now, therefore, be it RESOLVED, that the House of Representatives of the 82nd Texas Legislature hereby recognize October 26, 2011, as Texas Chicken Fried Steak Day and extend sincere best wishes to all who are taking part in this unique occasion."

The official holiday has passed, but you can still partake of the "beloved entrée" practically everywhere on Texas soil.

Mary's Café

Seventy miles west of Fort Worth and seventy
miles east of Abilene, the longtime reigning
champ of quintessential chicken-fried steak

119 Grant Ave.
Strawn, TX 76475
(254) 672-5741

Gristmill River Restaurant & Bar

A rising challenger located in an 1878 cotton gin with
a shady patio and views of the Guadalupe River

1287 Gruene Rd.
New Braunfels, TX 78130
(830) 625-0684
www.gristmillrestaurant.com

Zentner's Daughter Steak House

Chicken fried steak, the house specialty since the
eatery opened its doors in the mid-1970s

1901 Knickerbocker Rd.
San Angelo, TX 76904
(325) 284-3376
www.zentnersdaughter.com

Miller's Seawall Grill

Chicken-fried steak right across the street from the beach

1824 Seawall Blvd.
Galveston, TX 77550
(409) 763-8777
www.millersseawallgrill.com

Goodson's Cafe

Making world-famous chicken-fried steak since
it opened its doors in the mid-1950s

27931 Tomball Pkwy.
Tomball, TX 77377
(281) 351-1749
www.goodsonscafetomball.com

GET GIDDY
AT GILHOOLEY'S

Gilhooley's atmosphere may be curmudgeon, but its food offerings are quite amicable. For years it refused to accept credit cards and prohibited children; credit cards are now okay, but children are still out of luck. But that's what an eatery can do if the Travel Channel refers to it as the "ultimate seafood dive."

The no-frills restaurant's specialty is Oysters Gilhooley, a dozen pit-smoked oysters generously drenched in garlic butter and topped with Parmesan cheese, but the seafood joint also offers a fried oyster dinner, a fried oyster po'boy, barbecued oysters, a seasonal oyster stew, raw oysters, fried shrimp, barbecued crab, seafood cakes, and a full horseshoe-shaped bar—which is important because even grouchy regulars begrudgingly admit that everything on the menu goes well with a longneck beer and a side of hush puppies.

222 Ninth St.
San Leon, TX 77539
(281) 339-3813

GET YOUR DUE
AT DREW'S

A hole in the wall in West Fort Worth for years, Drew's Place has never tried real hard to be fancy, but don't let the function-over-form atmosphere fool you. Drew's calling card is mouthwatering soul food, comfort cuisine, and stick-to-your-ribs grub, par excellence. Because you've earned it.

Most eateries would be thrilled to enjoy universal appreciation for just one of their signature dishes, but Drew's bowls customers over with two. Drew's serves (1) the best fried chicken in Texas and (2) the best smothered pork chops in Texas. The restaurant also serves up a mean meat loaf, oxtail, collard greens, candied yams, steamed cabbage, and an excellent glass of sweet tea. And did I mention the desserts?

5701 Curzon Ave.
Fort Worth, TX 76107
(817) 229-9052

CHECK OUT
THE CZECH STOP

It used to be the only attention the small town of West received was for sitting near the site of the Crash at Crush, an 1896 Katy Railroad publicity stunt that involved the intentional collision of two railroad engines. These days the collision this community is most known for is culinary.

Not too long ago, when any normal, red-blooded Texan walked into a doughnut shop, all he or she saw on the menu was doughnuts (and maybe cinnamon rolls).

Talk about a culture shift.

Today, you can't find a doughnut shop that doesn't offer kolaches, and such eateries as the Czech Stop and Little Czech Bakery can take a lot of the credit. The deli/bakery thrills several hundred kolache-crazy customers a day, and they're open twenty-four hours a day, seven days a week.

104 S. George Kacir Dr.
West, TX 76691
(254) 826-4161
www.czechstop.net

EAT
AT THE OLD ORANGE CAFÉ

Located in the southwest center of downtown Orange (and just a few blocks from a crazy bend in the Sabine River), the Old Orange Café sits in the community's old dairy building, which closed down in 1948. Open for lunch every day except Saturday, it offers a mean country-fried steak, a tasty Cajun-smothered catfish, and a good assortment of burgers and sandwiches. The desserts are scrumptious, the service is down-home, and a marker-highlighted line around the interior walls indicates where the waters peaked during the last flood swell.

The Old Orange Café is worth a visit even if the Sabine is up. Just bring a life preserver.

914 W. Division Ave.
Orange, TX 77630
(409) 883-2233
www.oldorangecafe.com

HUMBLE YOURSELF
AT HERD'S

It used to be the only way you got a burger at Herd's Burgers in Jacksboro was how they served it. The hamburger meat was scooped, slung, and cooked to juicy perfection with a cement trowel, but the choice of sliced vegetables (usually lettuce, tomato, onion, and pickle) and condiments included on the burger was the cook's decision. The only side was a plain bag of potato chips. It was a Herd's Burger or no burger.

These days customers have some say as to what gets added to their juicy burgers, and they can select fries with their order instead of a bag of chips, but there's something really Texan about not being picky or finicky, and feeling nostalgic about the old Herd's (which opened in 1916) is okay. Of course, you can still leave the call to the cook. Regardless of menu evolution, Herd's Burgers is a Texas institution.

407 North Main St.
Jacksboro, TX 76458

GRAB A CHAIR
AT THE TEXAS CHILI PARLOR

Decisions, decisions, decisions. Habanero beef chili, black bean and sausage chili, white pork chili, five-bean veggie chili, or a three-bowl chili taster. Or a chili potato. Or Frito pie.

In a perfect world, every state would have its own chili parlor, and some do. In this imperfect world, at least we have our own, and it's been cooking up chili since 1976. This culinary landmark doesn't serve up deer chili, elk chili, or technically even traditional Texas chili—just mouthwatering variations on the theme—which is why the eatery is referred to as a parlor rather than a café or diner. Unlike most parlors, however, this one offers a well-stocked bar and stays open till 2:00 a.m.

Grab a stool and dig in. The Austin ambiance is on the house.

1409 Lavaca St.
Austin, TX 78701
(512) 472-2828
www.txchiliparlor.com

ROAD TRIPS

SPANISH FORT

When you see the town of Spanish Fort on a Texas map, it jumps out at you. It's tucked into a long bend of the Red River, just north of Nocona. You know—or at least think you know—that the Spanish didn't have any forts that far north in Texas. You wonder if the structure is still intact. You wonder why you've never heard of it before.

Your initial curiosity is rewarded by fascinating revelations.

First, the fort, which included wooden stockades, entrenchments, and a moat (yes, a moat—in Texas) is long gone. An Art Deco historical marker stands on the original location. Second, "Spanish" fort is wholly inaccurate. The fortification was actually a French structure built at the location of a preexisting Taovaya Indian village around 1719. The Taovaya had just moved into the region when the French were beginning to venture farther west along the Red River, and the two peoples quickly became successful trading partners. Third, when the only major defense of the fort was mounted in 1759, the attacking forces were actually Spanish, and the fort defenders were Taovaya, Wichita, and Comanche Indians joined and at least rudimentarily trained by a small French contingent. When an early Anglo settler visited the ruins one hundred years later, he simply assumed they were Spanish, hence the town name "Spanish Fort." Finally, the Native American rout of the Spanish at the French Taovaya fortress marked Spain's earliest defeat in Texas and probably kept them from expanding farther north.

The drive up from Nocona features hundreds of active oil industry pump jacks, and the site of Spanish Fort is intriguing but desolate—basically a ghost town itself.

Take FM 103 north out of Nocona.

INTREPID TEXAN

Many foreign and out-of-state (i.e., also foreign) visitors love taking pictures in front of and on the aforementioned oil industry pump jacks. Photography is fine, but *do not* climb or stand on the equipment. It engages and operates intermittently and sends no small number of tourists to the hospital (or grave) fairly regularly.

STATUE OF OLD YELLER

In classic Texas movies, such as *The Searchers*, the Lone Star State got credit for many panoramic vistas that weren't actually located here, but we give as good as we get.

Most people forget or never realized that *Old Yeller* was a Texas story. Its author, Fred Gipson, was born near Mason on February 7, 1908. As a young man, Gipson worked on several local farms and ranches until he enrolled at the University of Texas in 1933. His first book, *Fabulous Empire: Colonel Zack Miller's Story*, appeared in 1946, and his second book, *Hound-Dog Man*, came out in 1947. *Hound-Dog Man* was named to the popular Doubleday Book-of-the-Month Club and sold more than 250,000 copies in its first year. *Old Yeller* was published in 1956 and made into a successful Walt Disney film a year later. The motion picture portrayal of Old Yeller's passing is considered one of the saddest moments in cinematic history.

Mason County M. Beven Eckert Memorial Library
410 Post Hill St.
Mason, TX 76856

REGENCY
SUSPENSION BRIDGE

When you step onto the one-lane Regency Suspension Bridge, located at the intersection of Mills County Road 433 and San Saba County Road 137, it doesn't take long to figure out why they call the 340-foot structure the "swinging bridge." The wood-planked span moves under your weight, and then you watch, mouth agape, as cars and trucks drive across it.

The first bridge over the Colorado River at this spot was constructed in 1903, later collapsing under the weight of a crossing cattle herd. The second bridge was washed away by flooding in 1936. The structure we see today was a public works project completed in 1939, and it's one of the neatest little attractions in Texas.

Bypassed by modern, paved farm roads, reaching the Regency requires traversing miles of dirt road. When you finally get there, you should immediately cross the bridge in your sub-5,000 pound vehicle. Once you feel how much it moves under your individual weight, you may be disinclined to drive over it. Either way, once atop the bridge, you can survey a long stretch of the Colorado River from either side.

STAY
IN A SMALL TOWN

If you already live in a small town in Texas, visit another one. If you have already visited one, visit a second. Stay in the hotels or motels. Eat at the mom-and-pop restaurants, buy something from a small-town shop, support a local craftsperson. Meet the people, chat them up, and remember their faces—they're members of a vanishing breed.

SOME SMALL TOWNS TO VISIT

Archer City (Pop. 1,746)

The setting of the quintessential Texas film, *The Last Picture Show*, and hometown of *Lonesome Dove* author Larry McMurtry. McMurtry's fantastic Booked Up bookstore is located just off the main square.

www.bookedupac.com

Canadian (Pop. 2649)

Home of the magnificent Palace Theater, this High Plains oasis is near the Gene Howe Wildlife Management Area and the Black Kettle National Grasslands.

Iraan (Pop, 1,268)

Neat little town where V. T. Hamlin came up with the idea for the comic strip *Alley Oop*.

Bandera (Pop. 873)

Cowboy town with a dozen dude ranches.

Van Horn (Pop. 2,063)

If you're not planning on pitching a tent at Guadalupe Mountains National Park, Van Horn is a perfect base camp. Some decent hotels are available, and the El Capitan Hotel restaurant cooks up one the best steaks in Texas.

Palacios (Pop. 5,153)

Great little town located on Tres Palacios Bay, an arm of Matagorda Bay. Has a nice local museum and some good fishing spots.

Brackettville (Pop. 1,876)

The home of Fort Clark Springs and the Seminole Indian Scout Cemetery. Offers excellent access to the Kickapoo Caverns.

Marathon (Pop. 470)

Home of the well-known, singularly located Gage Hotel and a great stop on the way to Big Bend National Park.

RIVER ROAD
FROM PRESIDIO TO LAJITAS

This is the premier road trip in Texas, and it packs a wallop. Except for El Paso, folks who dwell in every other big city in Texas are somewhat insulated from practical reality of living in a border state. A large percentage of these people avoid spending time on the border, which is really a shame. It might disavow them of some of their misconceptions.

The River Road, also known as El Camino del Rio, runs right through the southern reaches of the relatively new 311,000-acre Big Bend Ranch State Park. This spectacular route is stark, dramatic, and picturesque. There's never a dull moment as the road climbs, twists, dips, and drops though the landscape, revealing startling vistas, teepee-shelter rest stops, hoodoo hikes, abandoned structures, a movie set, and sneak peeks of the elusive Rio Grande. Warnings not to cross the river demarcation abound, but gringos do it on tourist larks every day. The restored Fort Leaton is worth a stop, and the short but sensational Closed Canyon is a must-see, even when the temperatures are pushing 107°.

www.tpwd.texas.gov/state-parks/big-bend-ranch
www.tpwd.texas.gov/state-parks/fort-leaton

LOS EBANOS FERRY

There are few things Texans enjoy more than sticking their thumb in the eye of appointed or self-appointed arbiters of what's prim, proper, acceptable, or even advisable, and that's why crossing the Rio Grande at Los Ebanos is so awesome. Connecting Americans at the Rio Grande with Ciudad Diaz Ordaz in Mexico, the Los Ebanos ferry is the only remaining hand-pulled ferry in the United States. Known as *El Chalan*, the three-vehicle barge links the state of Texas with the Mexican state of Tamaulipas. The ferry runs from 8:00 a.m. to 4:00 p.m., seven days a week. A U.S. Border & Customs Service office (956-485-1084) operates on the American side of the ferry landing.

200 Flores St.
Los Ebanos, TX 78565

NEW LONDON
SCHOOL EXPLOSION

The state of Texas is no stranger to tragedies, mishaps, and catastrophic events, but the New London School Explosion on May 18, 1937, was particularly heartbreaking. At the time, the London School District was flush with oil and gas tax revenues and was one of the wealthiest districts in the nation. In fact, at their home football games, the London Wildcats faced opponents on the first gridiron in Texas to have electric lights. For some reason, however, school officials had foregone a traditional boiler heating system for six dozen gas heaters, and the gas pipes were leaking. When a shop instructor switched on an electric sander at 3:17 p.m., the resultant spark ignited the gas-air mixture. The massive explosion that followed killed more than three hundred students and teachers and injured another three hundred. Legendary Texas journalist Walter Cronkite's coverage of the explosion was his first national story.

London Museum and Cafe
10690 Main St.
Overton, TX 75684
(903) 895-4602

INTREPID TEXAN
One wall of the London Museum features a telegram
expressing condolences from Adolph Hitler.

ROY ORBISON MUSEUM

In April 1963, Roy Orbison signed on to tour the UK with a new, young English band that called themselves the Beatles. Upon his arrival, he quickly realized that even though he was better known and had had more success than the young Liverpool quartet, they were being advertised as the main draw. On opening night in Glasgow, Orbison agreed to play first and, after a dazzling set, began playing encores. After the first several encores, the Beatles stood stupefied backstage. After listening to the raucous crowd chant "We Want Roy!" again, after Orbison's fourteenth encore, the Beatles practically dragged him off the stage. Orbison would go on to be a close friend of the Beatles and continue stealing the spotlight from other iconic bands he toured with, including the Rolling Stones and the Beach Boys. His genius is immortalized in various legendary rock and roll mainstays, including "Only the Lonely," "Running Scared," "Crying," "Pretty Woman," and "Blue Bayou."

Not too shabby for a quiet, unassuming young man born in the small town of Vernon and raised in the smaller West Texas town of Wink (which Orbison described as "the middle of nowhere, 500 miles from everywhere"). Visitors come from all over the world to check out the little museum dedicated to him there and so should we all. Call in advance to schedule a visit.

213 Hendricks Blvd.
Wink, TX 79789
(432) 527-3441

BIG THICKET
NATIONAL PRESERVE

One of the most biodiverse areas in the world outside the tropics, the 105,000-acre Big Thicket National Preserve is best explored on foot and offers forty miles of trails to pursue that end. Home to 85 species of trees (including oak, sweet gum, beech, magnolia, pine, tupelo, and holly), the patchwork park protects 26 species of fern, 20 species of orchid, 185 species of birds, more than 50 species of reptiles, and at least 4 carnivorous plants.

During the Civil War, a considerable number of East Texas dissidents hid out in the Big Thicket to avoid being drafted by the Confederacy into what they considered "a rich man's war and a poor man's fight." In the spring of 1865, a Confederate captain burned down more than three thousand acres of the thicket in an unsuccessful attempt to flush out the dissidents.

Over the years, parts of the thicket have sheltered destitute families and purported "wild men," and some suggest it even provides a safe haven for Bigfoot. Bring beef jerky just in case.

Big Thicket National Preserve Visitors Center
6102 FM 420
Kountze, TX 77625
(409) 951-6700
www.nps.gov/bith/index.htm

INDIANOLA

Located on Matagorda Bay in Calhoun County, the ghost town of Indianola lies near where French explorer Robert Cavelier, Sieur de La Salle, landed in 1685, mistaking the bay there for the mouth of the Mississippi River. Indianola was founded in 1846 but demolished by a hurricane in 1875. The local citizenry rebuilt the town and the courthouse, but it was destroyed again by another hurricane in 1886 and subsequently abandoned. La Salle established Fort St. Louis near Garcitas Creek in Victoria County, but the venture was short lived, and the indigenous Karankawa burned the installation to the ground when the French left.

Not much of the Indianola community remains today, but a historical marker is near the original townsite as well as a forty-foot granite statue of La Salle overlooking the bay.

INTREPID TEXAN

The foundation of the second Calhoun County courthouse in Indianola can still be seen out in the water at low tide.

ROBERT E. HOWARD MUSEUM

Author Robert E. Howard was born in Peaster, went to high school in Brownwood, attended Howard Payne College, and spent most of his adult life in the little town of Cross Plains. But from his small corner of West Texas, he conquered civilizations, particularly as his most famous character, Conan the Barbarian. In his short, prolific career, Howard wrote mostly for pulp magazines but basically pioneered the sword and sorcery genre and is rivaled only by J. R. R. Tolkien in terms of his influence in the field of fantasy fiction. He was a friend and associate of horror writer H. P. Lovecraft and influenced legendary East Texas writer Joe R. Lansdale.

Today, Howard's Conan enjoys a pop-culture iconography not unlike that of Tarzan, Dracula, or Sherlock Holmes, and every summer Cross Plains hosts a Barbarian Festival in his honor.

625 SW Fifth St.
Cross Plains, TX 76443
(254) 725-6562
www.rehfoundation.org/the-robert-e-howard-house-and-museum

LEMON JEFFERSON
MEMORIAL CEMETERY

The grave in this cemetery (formerly known as the Wortham Negro Cemetery) that folks usually come to visit is the final resting place of blues legend and facility namesake Blind Lemon Jefferson. Though he typically gets less attention than his disciples, Huddie "Leadbelly" Ledbetter and Aaron Thibeaux "T-Bone" Walker, Jefferson was the first successful blues artist in America and is recognized as the father of Texas blues. His influence on popular music is probably impossible to quantify, especially in terms of later blues and rock artists, such as Sam "Lightnin'" Hopkins, Louis Armstrong, B. B. King, Carl Perkins, Bob Dylan, Jefferson Airplane, and the Beatles.

Jefferson died December 19, 1929, but his exact cause of death is unknown. When his body was returned to Texas, it was interred in an unmarked grave in Wortham. In 1967, he finally received a memorial.

When fans of Texas rock legend Buddy Holly visit his final resting place in Lubbock, they're encouraged to place guitar picks on his grave, but Jefferson's gravestone and his haunting, classic 1927 song "See That My Grave Is Kept Clean" clearly establish his position on the subject.

Located on the west side of State Hwy. 14
just north of Freestone County Rd. 1010.

PHOTO OPS

COWBOY CHRIST

A gravesite in Evergreen Cemetery near Paris, Texas, features a statue of Jesus (or an angel) that is wearing cowboy boots under his mantle. Whether you're a born-again Christian or borne away by alternate metaphysical interpretations, the booted deity (or disciple) is a nice touch, which will either make you smile and nod or smile and shake your head. It's a Texas thing, regardless.

560 Evergreen St.
Paris, TX 75460
(903) 784-6750

BALANCED ROCK
(BIG BEND)

The 2.2-mile round-trip Grapevine Hills Trail at Big Bend National Park doesn't have the star quality of the South Rim hike, the sex appeal of the Lost Mine Trail climb, or the stark beauty of the Santa Elena Canyon Trail, but what it lacks in drama it makes up for in serendipity. The moderate hike ends with three boulders perfectly placed to create a triangular window. The formation makes for decent shade and an almost comic interjection into an otherwise forbidding landscape.

STEVIE RAY VAUGHAN
STATUE

Stevie Ray Vaughan's first album, *Texas Flood* (1983), couldn't have been more appropriately titled. With his band, Double Trouble, Vaughan stormed the American music scene with a deluge of six-string virtuosity, practically single-handedly restoring the blues to the fore of the rock and roll music conversation and boosting the careers of neglected legends, such as B. B. King, Etta James, and Buddy Guy. Vaughan's bold, unshakable riffs fueled such signature hits as "Cold Shot," "Lovestruck Baby," "The Sky Is Crying," "Pride and Joy," "Life by the Drop," "Little Wing" (too many to name) and also lent considerable weight to David Bowie's best-selling album *Let's Dance* (1983). Then, of course, there's Vaughan's rendition of Hendrix's "Voodoo Child," where he arguably out-Jimi-ed Jimi himself.

At the time of his untimely demise in a helicopter crash in Wisconsin on August 27, 1990, Vaughan had inspired millions of fans and won the admiration of a number of his fellow guitar greats, including Keith Richards, Eric Clapton, and Jeff Beck. His influence is still expanding and, yes, the sky is still crying.

Auditorium Shores
Ann and Roy Butler Hike and Bike Trail
Austin, TX 78704

EARL CAMPBELL
STATUE

Three years after winning the Heisman Trophy and becoming the first pick in the 1978 NFL draft by the Houston Oilers, running back Earl Campbell was enshrined as an Official State Hero of Texas. His only three predecessors—Sam Houston, Davy Crockett, and Stephen F. Austin—had all been dead for more than a hundred years.

In a football state, Campbell was a man among boys at every level, leading Tyler's John Tyler High School to a state championship and the Texas Longhorns to a national title game. At the pro level, Campbell's combination of breakaway speed, agility, and power earned him NFL Offensive Rookie of the Year honors in 1978 and the Offensive Player of the Year award in each of his first three seasons. He also won the Associated Press MVP Award in 1979, was a five-time Pro Bowler and a three-time first-team All-Pro, and led the NFL in rushing (1978–1980) and rushing touchdowns (1979 and 1980).

Campbell was enshrined in the NFL Hall of Fame in 1991, and the nine-foot likeness of him sits in the southwest corner of Darrell K Royal–Texas Memorial Stadium.

405 E. Twenty-Third St.
Austin, TX 78712

AURORA CEMETERY
HISTORICAL MARKER

Who doesn't want a picture of themselves standing at the site of the first documented UFO crash in the United States?

The first official sighting of a flying saucer didn't occur in Roswell, New Mexico, in early July of 1947, and it wasn't conjured up on a movie set of *The Day the Earth Stood Still* in Century City, California, a few years later. New Mexico and Hollywood were late to the party. The first flying saucer was spotted by a farmer named John Martin in North Texas on January 22, 1878, and nineteen years later the first alien aircraft reportedly made unscheduled contact with Earth in the form of a spectacular crash on April 17, 1897. The pilot, who was assumed to be Martian, did not survive, and the citizens of Aurora respectfully interred him the next day, Easter morning, in their local cemetery.

507 Cemetery Rd.
Aurora, TX 76078

INTREPID TEXAN

The grave of the songwriter behind Willie Nelson's country western ballad "Pancho and Lefty" is just ten miles south at the Dido Cemetery in Pecan Acres. The Fort Worth native's name was Townes Van Zandt, and his inscription reads, "To Live's to Fly."

AURORA CEMETERY

THE OLDEST KNOWN GRAVES HERE, DATING FROM AS EARLY AS THE 1860s, ARE THOSE OF THE RANDALL AND ROWLETT FAMILIES. FINIS DUDLEY BEAUCHAMP (1825–1893), A CONFEDERATE VETERAN FROM MISSISSIPPI, DONATED THE 3-ACRE SITE TO THE NEWLY-FORMED AURORA LODGE NO. 479, A.F. & A.M., IN 1877. FOR MANY YEARS, THIS COMMUNITY BURIAL GROUND WAS KNOWN AS MASONIC CEMETERY. BEAUCHAMP, HIS WIFE CAROLINE (1829–1915), AND OTHERS IN THEIR FAMILY ARE BURIED HERE. AN EPIDEMIC WHICH STRUCK THE VILLAGE IN 1891 ADDED HUNDREDS OF GRAVES TO THE PLOT. CALLED "SPOTTED FEVER" BY THE SETTLERS, THE DISEASE IS NOW THOUGHT TO HAVE BEEN A FORM OF MENINGITIS.

LOCATED IN AURORA CEMETERY IS THE GRAVESTONE OF THE INFANT NELLIE BURRIS (1891–1893) WITH ITS OFTEN-QUOTED EPITAPH: "AS I WAS SO SOON DONE, I DON'T KNOW WHY I WAS BEGUN." THIS SITE IS ALSO WELL-KNOWN BECAUSE OF THE LEGEND THAT A SPACESHIP CRASHED NEARBY IN 1897 AND THE PILOT, KILLED IN THE CRASH, WAS BURIED HERE.

STRUCK BY EPIDEMIC AND CROP FAILURE AND BYPASSED BY THE RAILROAD, THE ORIGINAL TOWN OF AURORA ALMOST DISAPPEARED, BUT THE CEMETERY REMAINS IN USE WITH OVER 800 GRAVES. VETERANS OF THE CIVIL WAR, WORLD WARS I AND II, AND THE KOREAN AND VIETNAM CONFLICTS ARE INTERRED HERE.

(1976)

LIGHTNIN' HOPKINS
STATUE

The state of Texas's impact in the realm of blues music is no less seminal than its role in rock. The first major American blues artist was Coutchman native Blind Lemon Jefferson, and he mentored Louisiana legend Huddie "Leadbelly" Ledbetter in Dallas's Deep Ellum. Texas also produced Blind Willie Johnson, Aaron "T-Bone" Walker, Sippie Wallace, Clarence Gatemouth Brown, Albert Collins, Johnny "Guitar" Watson, Delbert McClinton, and Stevie Ray Vaughan. Besides Vaughan, the only Lone Star blues master who has a statue is Centerville native Sam "Lightnin'" Hopkins, who was a major influence on Jimi Hendrix, Billy Gibbons (of ZZ Top), and Creedence Clearwater Revival. At least a half-dozen other blues pioneers ought to have their own statues here in Texas, but we certainly won't turn our nose up at the one we have of Hopkins in Crockett.

200th block of S. Third St. in Crockett,
in a small park between Fannin and Goliad Avenues.

INTREPID TEXAN

The Slocum Massacre historical marker twenty-four miles north of Crockett on FM 2022 was the first marker in Texas to specifically acknowledge racial violence against African Americans. It was placed and dedicated on January 16, 2016.

GUADALUPE PEAK

Guadalupe Peak is the highest point in Texas, and getting there is no easy task. From the Pine Springs Visitor Center in the Guadalupe Mountains National Park, the 8.8-mile round-trip hike to the 8,749-foot peak involves a strenuous 2,927-foot gain in elevation, but once you arrive you're greeted by a steel pyramid at the summit and fantastic views all around, especially on a clear day. A photo or selfie with the commemorative spire in the background at this rarefied perch is quite something and an accomplishment you'll be glad you captured. And don't forget to retrieve the notebook from the small ammo box at the base of the steel spire and record your thoughts for future fellow climbers.

400 Pine Canyon Dr.
Salt Flat, TX 79847
(915) 828-3251
www.nps.gov/gumo/planyourvisit/pine-springs-visitor-center.htm

LIGHTHOUSE PEAK

A distinctive hoodoo formation near Capitol Peak in Palo Duro Canyon State Park, the Lighthouse stands three miles off the main park road. The Lighthouse Trail climbs nine hundred feet and offers little shade but is relatively moderate. The best place to get a picture is where the trail flattens out at the end of the first rise of the two-level ascent at the end of the hike.

Palo Duro Canyon State Park
11450 State Hwy. Park Rd. 5
Canyon, TX 79015
(806) 488-2227
www.tpwd.texas.gov/state-parks/palo-duro-canyon

SAM HOUSTON
STATUE

The sixty-seven-foot statue of Sam Houston standing on the east side of I-45 in Huntsville is the Lone Star State's Mount Rushmore. For Texas, Houston was George Washington, Thomas Jefferson (Houston was our first and third president), and Abraham Lincoln. Three out of four ain't bad.

For a general, a president, a senator, and a governor, Houston was also a keen contrarian. Though a Southern slave owner, he opposed Texas secession from the Union, warning that "the soil of our beloved South will drink deep the precious blood of our sons and brethren." Although he couldn't convince his fellow political representatives and citizens that they were committing a grave mistake in joining the Confederacy, he refused an offer from Lincoln to command a Union army to put down the Confederate forces in Texas. He couldn't stomach bearing arms against his neighbors.

INTREPID TEXAN

Howard Hughes, another Texas giant, is buried at Glenwood Cemetery in downtown Houston an hour south on Interstate 45 (depending on the traffic).

BUDDY HOLLY
STATUE

In the same way that American blues germinated and spread from the mastery of such artists as Blind Lemon Jefferson, rock and roll branched out and thrived from the artistry of Buddy Holly. John Lennon and Paul McCartney saw Holly when they were teenagers and based their music on his, later offering tribute to Holly's band the Crickets by naming their band the Beatles. Holly's *The Chirping Crickets* was the first album Eric Clapton ever purchased. At the age of thirteen, Elton John wore horned-rim glasses to imitate Holly, even though he didn't need them. Bruce Springsteen claimed that in the early days he always played Buddy Holly before he went on because it kept him honest. Keith Richards (of the Rolling Stones) put Holly's impact best when he said, "He's in everybody."

Holly's song list, which includes "Peggy Sue," "That'll Be the Day," "Oh Boy," and "True Love Ways," is timeless, and the raw footage of Holly and the Crickets performing "Peggy Sue" on the *Ed Sullivan Show* on December 1, 1957, still gives folks chills.

Holly's career came to an abrupt end on February 3, 1959, when he, J. P. "Big Bopper" Richardson, and Ritchie Valens were killed in a plane crash northwest of Mason City, Iowa.

1824 Crickets Ave.
Lubbock, TX 79401

INVASION
OF THE PICTURE SNAPPERS

Five species of blue legume grow in Texas: *Lupinus subcarnosus*, *Lupinus havardii*, *Lupinus concinnus*, *Lupinus perennis,* and *Lupinus plattensis*. Alternatively called a wolf flower, buffalo clover, and *el conejo*, Texans obsess over them every April. Otherwise normal folks begin pulling off on the sides of state highways or just plowing into the roadside gravel of farm roads. They jump out with cameras or phones with cameras and begin supervising poses and instructing their models, who vary in age from toddler to preteen and stand on two legs or four. The models sit, lie, smile, hug, and sometimes bark among the bluebonnets—the state flower.

And the cameras keep rolling.

PHOTO CREDITS

Page 90: Mission San Francisco de la Espada at Sunrise, courtesy: Carlos Noriega, Wikimedia Commons

Page 91: Guadalupe Peak summit 2005-03-12, courtesy: Geoffrey J. King, Wikimedia Commons

Pages 92–93: Padre Island National Seashore Truck, courtesy: E. R. Bills

Page 94: A statue of rock-'n'-roll legend Buddy Holly, the centerpiece of a walk of fame that honors other West Texas musicians in Holly's hometown of Lubbock, Texas, courtesy: Carol M. Highsmith, Wikimedia Commons

Page 95: A portion of a classic, now-abandoned, western-movie and music-video set in what is now the ghost town of Contrabando in Big Bend Ranch State Park in Brewster County, Texas , courtesy: Carol M. Highsmith, Wikimedia Commons

Pages 96–97: Boots on the fence, courtesy: NorthcottPhotos, Wikimedia Commons

Page 98: USS *Texas*, courtesy: Texas Historical Commission, The Portal to Texas History

Page 107: Immaculate Conception Church Brownsville Texas, courtesy: 25or6to4, Wikimedia Commons

Page 111: Janis Joplin seated 1970, courtesy: Albert B. Grossman Management, Wikimedia Commons

Page 115: Katherine Stinson with her biplane, courtesy: Bain News Service, Wikimedia Commons

Page 120: L&J sign, courtesy: E. R. Bills

Page 134: Demdo Factor, courtesy: E. R. Bills

Page 145: New London School Cenotaph, Shutterstock

Page 147: Aankomst Roy Orbinson (Amerikaanse zanger) op Schiphol Roy Orbinson, courtesy: Jack de Nijs / Anefo, Wikimedia Commons

Page 152: Statues of Jesus, some say this is an unidentified angel, are not unusual in American cemeteries. Nor are monuments like this one at the grave of small-town businessmen. What makes the statue at this final resting place of Willet Babcock in Paris's Evergreen Cemetery unusual and uniquely "Texas" are the cowboy boots that the robed figure depicted is wearing, courtesy: Carol M. Highsmith, Wikimedia Commons

Page 159: Aurora TX Cemetery Marker, courtesy: E. R. Bills

Page 167: Buddy Holly Brunswick Records, courtesy: Brunswick Records, Wikimedia Commons

INDEX